The Christian's Dream Guide

A New Framework for Understanding Dreams

Tyler Wolfe

Book design by Jason Hassig
Illustrations by Gershom Wetzel at Aoristos
http://aoristos.com/

Readers should be aware that Internet Web sites offered as citations may
have changed or disappeared between the time this was written and when it
is read.

Scripture references are from the New American Standard Version. Copy-
right 1960, 1962, 1963, 1968, 1971, 1972, 1975, 1977, 1995, The Lockman
Foundation. Used by permission
All rights reserved.
ISBN-10: 1492884081
ISBN-13: 978-1492884088

DEDICATION

This book is dedicated to my friends and family at Trinity Church, Cedar Hill, Texas. Thank you for helping me achieve my dreams.

CONTENTS

PREFACE

I am sometimes asked how I started writing books and interpreting dreams. Many people are not aware this is a gift and ministry of the Holy Spirit. I was no exception. Until I was an adult I had never heard of anyone interpreting dreams until I saw a video of John Paul Jackson doing it. As I watched, he began to relate a dream in which he was pregnant and told he would give birth to "seers" who would minister under an anointing allowing them to understand visions and dreams. Until that time I had not heard of a seer, but in the past God had spoken to me in visions and dreams and I could understand them. After watching the video I began to have an increase in God given dreams that were directional for my life. I was finishing my degree in Education and working in the facilities ministry of a large church. Although I was busy I was stirred by the Holy Spirit to speak with people about their meaningful dreams.

I did not attend a school for instruction on how to do it. I operated on the gift alone. I would spend time in prayer and Bible study then go interpret. Upon hearing a dream the interpretation would pour out of me, like prophecy. I had a strong anointing in this area so I interpreted precociously. I had spoken with hundreds of people over the course of a few months. The majority were non-Christians so I started to evangelize. I found people wanted to understand their dreams, but the secular information available to them didn't help. The market was filled with misinformation.

Around this time, the Holy Spirit began to speak to me through dreams and prophets about collecting the symbolism in the Bible and creating a website. The words spoken to me were specific. God wanted to do something "significant with me because of my character." My website christiandreamsymbols.com and the subsequent editions of the Biblical Dream Symbols Dictionary are a scion of those prophetic encounters. This book is also the result of acting upon a prophetic word. As I began, I heard the Holy Spirit tell me this was our book; we would write it together. Because of this, I am confident this work will bear the imprimatur of Christ and greatly benefit The Body of Christ.

Something I learned while being ministered to by the prophetic revivalist Keith Miller is that the anointing a person has is transferable. It is my prayer that everyone who reads this book be gifted and anointed by the Lord Jesus Christ to better understand their dreams and interpret the dreams of others. *May you be greatly enriched by his power and love, according to the Father's purposes and will.*

Tyler Wolfe

INTRODUCTION

This book is designed to introduce the reader to a framework for understanding and interpreting dreams. It is only recently that researchers have been able to uncover the neural substrate for our dreams. The recent and significant work with neuropsychological and neuroimaging studies has demystified some of the long standing questions about this subject. This book attempts to integrate this information into the curriculum of Christian dream interpretation.

The framework emphasizes establishing objective criteria for determining the origin of a dream. This is necessary because dreams from God are the only dreams the Bible endorses us to act upon. Therefore, it is imperative we guarantee His authorship before assigning biblical meaning to a dream. The biblically-supported-propositions of this framework are:

1. Dreams originate from three sources: The mind, God and demons.

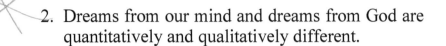

2. Dreams from our mind and dreams from God are quantitatively and qualitatively different.

3. The majority of our dreams do not come from God.

Because this framework integrates the current scientific research on dreams, Chapter One must start with a basic overview of that research. It covers the mechanisms at work while we sleep and how dreams are studied. It also covers some early major contributors to the study of dreams. Chapter Two will use information from neuropsychological and neuroimaging studies to answer the most difficult questions about our dreams. Chapter Three consists of a presentation of the biblical evidence supporting the framework. It also includes a critique of the position that demons cannot cause or affect a person's dreams.

Chapter Four introduces the reader to the principles of dream analysis. It will also show you what to expect if you choose to evangelize by interpreting dreams for others. Chapter Five contains case studies of prototype dreams. This will help the reader to become proficient in interpretation by using the core concepts that guide the thinking of experts within a domain.

The subject of dreams is broad. It encompasses diverse theories with little common ground. This book is not intended to be comprehensive. It is designed to concisely introduce and integrate the information presented within it.

1

THE SCIENCE OF SLEEP

If you want to understand dreams, you must have an understanding of the processes at work while we sleep. Dreams are a cognitive process which can be used as a mode of communication between God and man. Although God uses dreams to speak with us, the primary mode of communication between God and man is the Bible. If you do not understand the processes involved when you dream, you may not recognize a dream that comes from the mind. Many people come to me for an interpretation of a dream they find ambiguous, believing it to be from God, when the true source is their own mind. An understanding of the science of dreams makes it easier to recognize one's own mind at work during sleep.

 This chapter will introduce you to some common facts about sleeping and dreaming and the mechanisms at work during both. I will also introduce the way dreams are examined by the scientific community. It will end with an introduction to some of the beliefs about dreams from ancient origins and explain the significance of a few recent contributors as well.

REALITIES OF SLEEP

The average person spends at least a third of their lives sleeping.[1] To put this in perspective, if you were to live to the age of seventy you would have spent over 200,000 hours sleeping. Faced with those numbers it is easy to feel as though you should be more productive, but sleeping this much is normal. Human beings have a circadian rhythm.[2] This is the natural, twenty-four hour cycle that regulates our need for wakefulness and sleep. It is controlled by our brain and regulated by a combination of internal and external factors including how much light or darkness we get. It is the reason we feel jet lag and why we feel tired around the same time every day.[3] It is an internal clock given to us by God to govern rest and periods of alertness. Anyone can attest to feeling more alert during certain periods of the day than others and this is frequently attributed to your circadian rhythm.

Every person has a unique optimal time when their body is ready to go to sleep.[4] We also have a time around two hours before we go to sleep that is our most alert period of the day called the "sleep gate."[5] It is thought that we are most alert so that the brain can make an easy transition to sleep.[6] Researchers believe we are being primed for a period of rest.

The amount of sleep a person needs can vary greatly by individual, but a person will die if they go too long without it entirely.[7] Although this is true, people have gone

2

extended periods without it, and after a full eight hours of rest, recover without any known long-term problems.[8]

THE STAGES OF SLEEP

When we sleep, we go through four, continuously-deeper stages in which the brain becomes quieter but the body may move. These four stages are marked by progressively slower brain waves.[9] In a fifth stage called REM sleep, the brain is highly active, but the body is paralyzed. This is why it is considered different than the other four stages.[10] REM stands for rapid eye movement because our eyes are darting back and forth under our eyelids.[11] As adults, REM accounts for around 20-25 percent of the time we are asleep during an eight-hour period. We do not stay in REM continuously; we cycle through the stages of sleep and go back into REM about every 90 minutes.[12]

Sleep Cycle

Stage 1	Stage 2	Stage 3	Stage 4	REM
4-5%	45-55%	4-5%	10-15%	20-25%
Sleep onset. Muscle activity slows down.	Breathing and Heart rate slows.	Deep Sleep. EEG starts to show slow delta waves.	Very deep sleep.	Rapid eye movement. Muscle paralysis. Mind becomes very active.

The REM stage is what we associate with dreaming.[13] Dreaming is normal except in certain medical cases involving brain injury.[14] There are famous cases involving people who have experienced brain injury resulting in an absence of REM for the remainder of their life, but functioned normally.[15] On average, adults have between four and six dreams per night and most of them are not remembered at all.[16] In fact 95-99 percent of all dreams are forgotten.[17] The content and frequency of dreaming is different for children than that of adults.[18] Complex dream content requires that areas of our brain that affect our ability to use visuospatial skills to be mature.[19] If you think of your brain as a computer then visuospatial skills are similar to software that creates videogame landscapes. That software is missing until a certain time as the code is being written. Spatial skills are what allow us to produce a complex internal dream image. Because of this, children do not begin to have adult-like dream content until adolescence or their early teens.[20]

There are also differences in the dreams of the blind. People born blind do not see images in their dreams.[21] Those who go blind between the ages of five to seven have visual images in their dreams.[22] This is because they went blind after the areas in the brain that affect visuospatial skills developed. It is the research with the blind that proves visual imagery in dreams is a gradual cognitive ability developed over several years. For this reason, researchers now take the stance that very young children do not dream.[23] This fact has been somewhat controversial. Infants spend a large amount of time in REM and it was previously assumed they were dreaming.

4

DREAM RESEARCH

Dream research is usually conducted in a sleep lab at hospitals or universities where they attach subjects to a machine called an electroencephalogram (EEG) that records brain waves while subjects sleep.[24] Subjects are awakened throughout the night during different stages of the sleep cycle by lab technicians and asked questions such as whether they were dreaming and what it was about.[25] This information is catalogued using a system of content analysis and used in various scientific studies.[26]

EEG Machine

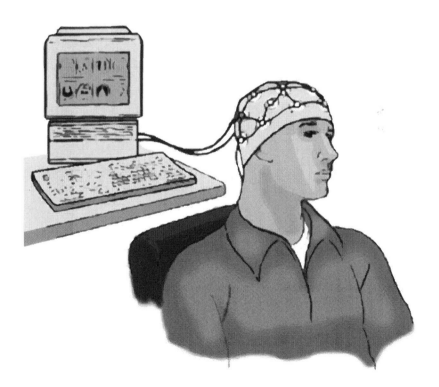

Dream research can also be carried out without sleeping in a lab. In this method, researchers ask participants to sleep in their own homes and record their dreams in a journal in the morning.[27] There is some controversy as to which method yields the best results. Some people complain that people are conscious of being watched by researches in a lab. They argue it influences what people report. For instance, if you had a sexual dream you may not want to tell a stranger about it. Despite this objection, lab dream reports are still used and seen as a viable source of information.

The content analysis of a dream report is one of the main focuses of research. Content analysis is an objective, quantitative approach to dissecting a dream based on a number of scales, activities of the dreamer and emotions.[28] Quantitative analysis allows researchers to see whether a certain emotion, anger, for example, is represented within a demographic and then draw conclusions backed by hard numbers about what people typically dream about. We know that men dream about sex more often than women and that houses are the number one setting for our dreams.[29] We also know that animal dreams make up less than 10 percent of all adult dreams. Out of that, dogs and horses are the two most frequently reported.[30]

MILESTONES OF DREAM RESEARCH

Theories about our dreams changed with the invention of scientific equipment that allowed researchers to understand the underlying processes of our minds. Prior to this our understanding of dreams came from a religious or philosophical point of view. REM sleep was discovered in 1953 by Dr. Nathaniel Kleitman and Dr. Eugene Aserinsky while examining the eyelids of sleeping research subjects.[31] This discovery spurred research by Dr. William C. Dement. Dement described the cycles of sleep and established the relationship between REM and dreaming.[32] Around the same time as Dement, another researcher named Michel Jouvet identified REM as a stage of brain activity separate from sleep and wakefulness.[33] Jouvet labeled this "paradoxical sleep" because although we were resting, our mind was highly active.[34]

Another important step in our understanding of dreams took place in 1977. Researchers J. Allan Hobson and Robert McCarley proposed the activation-synthesis theory of dreaming. This theory explained the physiological processes of dreaming by showing how circuitry in the brain became active and sent signals to other areas.[35] This was important because it gave us an empirical basis for theories about dreams to emerge. Since the turn of the century, psychoanalysts spent considerable time evaluating people's dreams. The activation-synthesis theory was a subtle suggestion that psychoanalysis was useless. In essence, dreams where not intentional, they were just our brain trying to make sense of random neurons firing.

EARLY THEORIES

Religious and spiritual systems of dream interpretation have probably existed as long as people have been baffled by their dreams. The archeological record shows that human beings have held a belief in the impact of dreams for thousands of years.[36] People of the past practiced "dream incubation." This was a ritual in which a person would sleep in a sacred place (like a temple) in the hopes of speaking to a spirit or deity.[37] All the information gleaned from the spirit would help the person find an answer to their problems or garner healing for an ailment. The Greeks and Romans had numerous temples where people could sleep in the hopes of speaking with a spirit in a dream.

The belief that spirits can cause someone to have a dream has been around at least 5000 years and dream incubation is still practiced by people around the world today.[38] People of the past also believed that dreams could come from our own psyche, but the predominate belief about dreams was that they were a mode of communication between man and a spirit world.[39] Even today, the most widely held beliefs about dreams have their roots in ancient mysticism.[40]

EARLY DREAM THEORISTS

The early dream theorist most people are familiar with is Sigmund Freud. Freud was born in 1856 and worked as neurologist before he became famous for writing about dreams.[41] Freud believed dreams had the function of guarding our sleep from being interrupted.[42] He also believed that dreams were a form of "wish fulfillment" and all dreams contained memories from the day's events that he called "day residue."[43] Freud's most notorious assumption was that many adult dreams were sexual wishes in disguise.[44] Freud's ideas about dreams were grounded in the construct of the unconscious. This is an area of the mind thought to influence our waking motives and dreams.[45]

For Freud, dreams had two levels. The dream itself was called the *manifest content* the hidden message disguised within was called the *latent content*.[46] Freud would attempt to find the hidden meaning of dreams through the use of free association. In this technique the dreamer speaks what comes to mind while reflecting upon the dream. This is supposed to help uncover the dreams' true meaning.[47] For instance, if I had a dream in which my mother and I were speaking at the kitchen table, Freud might say the word "mother" and I would say the first thing that came to mind. Working backward down the psyche allows him to unscramble the latent content of the dream.

For Freud, the symbols in a dream had a single, consistent meaning. For instance, a snake was a penis and nothing else.[48] For other interpreters, snakes could mean multiple things. Freud propagated his beliefs and defended them fiercely. He was a great writer who wrote volumes over the course of his life. Although he is thought of as the father of modern dream interpretation, he was not original in his thinking. He took ideas about dreams that had been around for some time and made them his own. He did, however, make a good observation that many dreams are traceable to things we have done during our waking hours. This observation is called a "continuity principle."[49] Freud's belief that our waking actions could be influenced by our unconscious also has merit. These two beliefs may be the kernels of truth within Freud's theory of the dream work. Although Freud is credited with being the father of dream interpretation, his lasting contribution to the subject is minimal. The most influential early dream theorist is Carl Jung.

Carl Gustav Jung was a Swiss psychiatrist and friend of Freud, but he split with him over issues of dream theory and began developing work on his own ideas.[50] Jung was highly educated and combined multiple disciplines to form his beliefs about dreams.[51] Jung spent over five years attempting to explore his own unconscious through the examination of his dreams.[52] In the course of this he claimed to encounter a winged creature with horns named Philemon who told him he could help Jung attain knowledge about things people could not normally gain access to.[53] It was during this time that Jung's primary concepts about dreams were forged.

Jung believed dreams were the product of a "collective unconscious." The collective unconscious is an inherited collection of experiences that cause human beings to perceive things as mythological shapes or patterns.[54] Jung called these patterns "archetypes." He believed the archetypes were symbolic and the focus of Jungian dream analysis was on interpreting the symbols.[55] The symbols in a dream did not have a concrete meaning to Jung like they did for Freud. A snake may have many meanings in Jungian dream theory.[56] Another way of understanding Jung's theory of the collective unconscious and the archetypes is by thinking of them as animal instincts. Instincts cause an animal to act a certain way without thinking. The collective unconscious is a type of preprogrammed human knowledge that affects the way we perceive things. It is the genetically passed-down mental remains of our species' ancient past.[57]Jung saw dreams as an expression of archetypes and underdeveloped areas of our personality. This was something he called "compensation."[58] For Jung, dreams could help you achieve a balance in your life by showing you areas you needed to work on. Dreams compensated for misunderstood beliefs and fears that left a person developmentally stuck.[59]

Although Jung never published a systematic study of his beliefs on dreams his ideas are in wide use today. My experience with the general public confirms Jung's lasting influence in dream theory.

2

A CONTEMPORARY VIEW OF DREAMS

This chapter will introduce you to a contemporary understanding of our dreams. With the advances in neuroimaging equipment we have mapped significant portions of the brain while we dream. This understanding of the way our mind and body work has been incorporated into all contemporary dream theories.

There is not one single theory that can answer every question about our dreams. Although all theories reveal the biases of those who support them, some modern scientific dream research results contain useful information concerning this subject. The sections that follow are based on some of the latest scientific research about dreaming. Note that the material contains hypotheses and conclusions based on various research, some of which hold competing theories. If a statement or conclusion is not referenced, it is my opinion.

THE GREAT DEBATE

Contemporary dream theorists are divided over the argument of function. Nearly all of them believe dreams have meaning, but not all of them believe dreams have a function. This is an important distinction. Function means that dreams have a task or purpose. A good way to understand this argument is by comparing it to the male nipple. Nipples on a woman secrete milk, but nipples on a man don't do anything. In other words, they serve no function. Although this sounds trivial, it is difficult to prove claims about our dreams serving a purpose. As we have seen in the last chapter, beliefs about dreams are myriad and steeped in conjecture. The quest to empirically prove the purpose of our dreams serves to discredit the intractable ideas clouding the truth of this subject.

Theorists that believe dreams have a function can be classified as physiological or psychological. Physiological theories are founded on ideas that dreams allow us to use different connections in our brain that affect certain types of learning and creativity.[1] Others believe dreams evolved as a way to mentally rehearse every day activities to better prepare us for threatening situations.[2] An example of this is when cavemen needed to prepare themselves for running from predatory animals. They could safely practice this in a dream and be better prepared the next day if such an event did occur.

Psychological ideas are based on the belief that the function of dreams is to allow human beings to work out our problems from the day and our worrisome social interactions.[3] In this way, dreams act as a mode of catharsis. In psychoanalytic theory, catharsis is an emotional release of unconscious conflicts.[4] This is where the belief that dreams play a role in stress relief comes from. Some researchers like to combine psychological and physiological theories. They believe sleep and dreaming play roles in memory, learning and in keeping us in a healthy mental state.[5]

The most prevalent theory denying any function for our dreams is the updated version of the activation-synthesis model discussed in the last chapter under the acronym AIM. AIM is a three dimensional model used to visualize the various states of consciousness of the brain.[6] Proponents of AIM believe dreams to be the brains' way of trying to make sense of random neurons firing while we sleep.[7] It is not infrequent to hear people only familiar with the older activation-synthesis model saying that "dreams mean nothing." Although AIM does not teach that dreams are meaningless it does consider them to be incoherent and purposeless, reducing them to a sort of night-time delirium.[8]

Another well-supported theory denying a function for our dreams is called the neurocognitive model. The neurocognitive model utilizes the neuroimaging findings of people who have damage to specific parts of their brain in order to reveal the parts not necessary for dreaming.[9] Let me describe how this works. Say you want to pinpoint the parts of your car that are necessary to keep it running when the engine is turned on. You could do this by opening the hood and systematically disconnecting one thing at a time to see if the car still ran. You pull one plug and the car still runs. You pull another and it shuts off. Using brain lesion studies is a great way to be exact about what is needed and what is not. The main idea behind the neurocognitive model is that, although dreams are coherent and meaningful, they can be seen as a form of night-time mind wandering with similarities to waking thought.[10]

Theorists debate how the mind actually forms a dream and which centers are fully involved, but they agree that the basic structures are clear.[11] In the next section I discuss what centers of the brain are active when we dream and how those areas are thought to affect the content.

THE MECHANISMS OF REM SLEEP

When we are in REM sleep our brain is highly active but our body is paralyzed. Our body is able to do this by stopping the release of certain neurotransmitters.[12] Neurotransmitters are chemicals that transmit signals between neurons.[13] Neurons are cells that process and transmit information via electrical and chemical means. We have billions of neurons in our brain.[14] You can think of neurons like a network of roads and highways that crisscross a large city allowing information to be transferred from one place to another. One neurotransmitter our body stops is histamine. Histamine increases wakefulness and prevents sleep.[15] This is why antihistamines like Benadryl® cause drowsiness. Our body thinks it's time for bed.

Neuron Cell

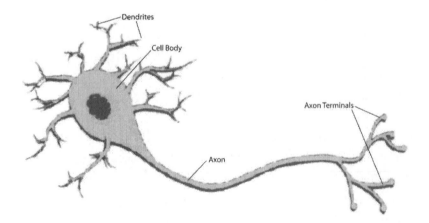

Although there is evidence that the hypothalamus may control REM it is currently accepted that neurons in the pons, an area of the brain stem, are active during REM and thought to be responsible for initiating it.[16] From the pons, signals are sent to the thalamus, which acts as a gatekeeper for signals being sent to other parts of the brain. During REM, parts of the brain associated with processing visual information, emotion and learning are all very active.[17] Although we can have dreams during other stages of sleep it is agreed upon that the REM stage supports our ability to have our most vivid and lengthy dreams.[18]

THE DEFAULT STATE OF OUR MIND

Some of the best supported evidence suggests dreaming is a product of a default network or "resting state"[19] The default mode is the setting that our brain reverts to when we are not engaged in goal-directed tasks whether we are asleep or awake. Evidence suggests that wakeful fantasizing, like daydreaming and mind-wandering, are products of the default network.[20] Both of these are undirected, spontaneous thoughts that consist of our current concerns, social interactions and long-term memories.[21] Why we revert to daydreaming is not completely known, but one of the reasons people like to fantasize is that we enjoy it. Imaginative processes are not distinguished from real ones. They make use of the same systems in our brain used to experience real pleasure.[22] Fantasizing is the default setting of our mind when we read a story. We put ourselves inside of it.[23] We enjoy fantasizing about being a professional athlete or celebrity. Because of the similarities revealed by neuroimaging studies between waking mind-wandering and dreaming; dreams may constitute an amplified version of undirected, spontaneous thought.[24] In essence, dreams can be explained as a type of thinking while asleep.

THE DREAMING BRAIN

It is thought that the dreaming brain may be active in many areas that parallel waking consciousness with the exclusion of the executive centers of the brain.[25] The executive centers of the brain are in the frontal lobe and help guide your behavior when you are awake including decision making and self-control. This is the area we associate with our personality and self-will.[26] The executive centers are suppressed during REM.[27] It is thought that the turning off our "self" is why we do things in our dreams we would never do while awake. There is very little moral restraint in our dreams. This is why we wake up feeling humiliated at the unsavory actions of our dream selves. Although the executive centers of the brain are turned off, the mind may turn on a few areas in the frontal lobe critical to cognitive processing, but our "ego" or "self" is still suppressed.

Another area of great importance is that of the limbic system, especially the amygdala and hippocampus, which control the storage and retrieval of memories and emotions.[28] The limbic system controls our "fight or flight" mechanisms while we are awake. It is the reason we startle when we think we see a snake that turns out to be a stick. It is the seat of powerful emotions like fear, anger and anxiety. The amygdala is highly active during REM and probably responsible for the retrieval of emotionally relevant dream content.[29]

Areas of the Brain Affecting Dream Content

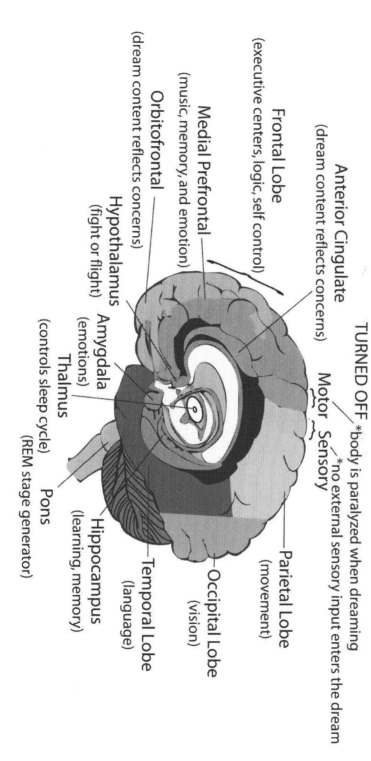

Anterior Cingulate
(dream content reflects concerns)

Frontal Lobe
(executive centers, logic, self control)

Medial Prefrontal
(music, memory, and emotion)

Orbitofrontal
(dream content reflects concerns)

Hypothalamus
(fight or flight)

Amygdala
(emotions)

Thalmus
(controls sleep cycle)

TURNED OFF
*body is paralyzed when dreaming
*no external sensory input enters the dream

Motor Sensory

Parietal Lobe
(movement)

Occipital Lobe
(vision)

Temporal Lobe
(language)

Hippocampus
(learning, memory)

Pons
(REM stage generator)

17

THE FUNCTION OF DREAMS

If dreams have a function the best evidence in support of this is in the area of learning. In one study, people taught a skill and then deprived of REM sleep could not remember certain skills that they had learned.[30] Another experiment showed that test subjects who slept for at least six hours after learning a new task improved when they did that task again, whereas those who did not sleep did not improve. Researchers also found that those who improved the most slept for a full eight hours.[31]

The reason getting eight hours of sleep plays a vital role in memory and learning is that we are able to cycle through all of the stages of sleep. Cycling through the stages is critical. There is a two-step process for the memories crucial to learning becoming consolidated and incorporated into the brain.[32] The two regions of the brain involved with this process are the hippocampus and neocortex. The hippocampus is in charge of storing recent memories and the neocortex is where old, permanent memories are located.[33] During non-REM, slow brain-wave stages, the hippocampus plays its records for the neocortex. During REM the process switches and the neocortex plays its records back to the hippocampus. Once a new memory from the hippocampus is connected to an older existing memory the neocortex tells the hippocampus to erase the memory.[34]A full eight hours of sleep ensures this process is complete.

Another experiment conducted by the same researchers used the video game Tetris to see if the brain uses dreaming to reinforce learning.[35] The game Tetris involves stacking falling blocks in the right sequence in order to score points. The experiment was carried out during the first hour of sleep called "hypnagogic" sleep. This means we are not fully awake or asleep. In the study, experimenters used three sets of participants. One group were expert Tetris players, another novices, and the last amnesiacs (anterograde amnesiacs do not have short-term memory due to damage to the hippocampus).[36] The experiment found that various subjects saw falling blocks in their dreams, but the majority saw these images on the second night of the experiment. It is thought that the brain was doing this as a delayed reaction. Researchers speculate that if the subject matter we are dealing with is difficult, the need to learn pushes the brain into dreaming about it.[37] The finding that dreaming supports learning was again confirmed when the novices who were the worst at the game were also the ones who reported seeing the falling blocks during sleep-onset. The more we need help learning something the more the brain reviews that information.[38]

The results of these experiments suggest that the early part of sleep is dedicated to dreaming about things we need to learn.

WHAT DO WE DREAM ABOUT?

This is an area of division between empiricists and Jungian practitioners. Empiricists believe there is continuity between dreams and our waking life. Jungian analysts believe dreams express aspects of our personality that are underdeveloped. I often hear people steeped in the tradition of Jungian interpretation say that dreams reflect "compensation," the opposite of your personality, but this is dubious.

"...the idea seems to be contradicted by every relevant systematic study since the beginning of modern-

Dreams come from last 16 hours of awaken K6

day dream research in the late 19th century, when psychologists who wrote down their own dreams found considerable continuity between dream content and waking cognition."[39]

The continuity-principle is the one supported by objective measures. Studies show the majority of our dreams are taken from the last sixteen hours of our waking life.[40] We dream about the things that are most important to us.[41] About half can be traced directly to our lived experiences.[42] Our negative social interactions, fears and pleasurable memories are frequently expressed. Overall, dreamers report more negative ones than positive.[43] In fact, several large studies showed only 20 percent of dreams were positive ones.[44] If you have an emotionally upsetting experience you are likely to have a dream about it.[45] If you spend considerable time trying to figure out the answer to a problem, you may dream about it. One researcher joked that if there was a mathematical equation to determine if we will dream about something, it might be time spent thinking about a topic multiplied by how emotionally important it is.[46]

(Time Spent Thinking x Emotion = Dream)

Research also shows that what we dream about changes as we age. Children dream of animals more frequently and have less developed storylines.[47] We also know that the vast majority of dreams are in color in children and adults.[48] Although we have a good record of what we dream about, it does not explain why our dreams are not a representation of our actual memories. They are not a recording, but a surreal distortion. The answer may be that they are coming from a different type of memory.

THE MEMORY SOURCES OF OUR DREAMS

One of the things learned in the experiment with the Tetris playing amnesiacs was dreams do not come from the declarative memory system in the hippocampus. Declarative memories are recent memories that you guarantee you know, like the name of your wife or what you ate for breakfast.[49] We know declarative memories are not used because amnesiacs reported seeing falling blocks in the images of their dreams and they have damage to the hippocampus. Instead, we may be accessing implicit memories for dream images.[50] Implicit memories fall into two categories, semantic and procedural. Procedural memories are things you can do without explaining how you do them, like riding a bicycle. Semantic memories are general facts, like remembering what a cat looks like. When we dream we are given pieces of things from our recent memories, but the details of the event are unavailable. The way this unfolded in the experiment was that the amnesiacs could remember seeing falling blocks, but concrete information like the desks in the room and the computer were not seen.

Implicit memories are not anchored to concrete times, places and details.[51] The use of implicit memories explains why some dreams are single images, without story-like qualities to them. To understand implicit dream images you need to rely on intuition (knowing something to be true even when you can't explain how). An example of what an implicit memory would look like is a dream in which a woman saw a singular image of a girl with a blue coat standing in front of her and pitch black everywhere else. Like the falling blocks in Tetris the memory of the girl is not anchored to the rest of the details of the event.

Damage to the hippocampus can account for the absence of declarative memories in dreaming which may explain why dreams are not an exact recording of an event, but there are other factors affecting the illogical appearance of our dreams as well.

WHY DREAMS APPEAR ILLOGICAL

Some researchers teach that images in dreams are designed to match the dominate emotion from the memory they are associated with. This is called "contextualization."[52] Another way to understand contextualization is with an illustration. My friend told me he was once chased by a small dog on his way to his grandmother's house. As the dog barked and charged at him from the porch of its owner's house, my friend was startled, dropped his bag and ran. Later, he reported having a dream in which he was being chased by a pit-bull. In this way his mind gave him images that more accurately reflected the emotions he felt. A little dog would hardly elicit the stark terror he initially felt while being chased, so his mind substituted a pit-bull. Contextualization is your brain giving you a picture of what you have defined as a vicious dog in place of the actual memory. Researchers think it is possible that when we dream, our emotions, determine the images we see.[53] If the dominate emotion of a memory is stress, our mind finds an image that conveys that emotion. When we are awake it is the other way around. What we think and see causes us to experience an emotion.

It is thought that the mind is able to add the correct context by suppression of the left-hemisphere of the brain during dreaming. The left-hemisphere is associated with logic, rational thinking and problem solving, and is active during non-REM.[54] The right-hemisphere is associated with how we perceive visual and auditory input.[55] The right brain identifies an object by function and purpose. It is also "responsible for processing associations."[56] Another way of looking at it is the left-half of the brain tells you the name of the object you are looking at is a "cup" while the right-half tells you its function: "you drink out of this."[57] If you have damage to your right-hemisphere, you could see a cup and give the title of it, but you could not tell what it did. Our dreams appear illogical because the images are defined by what we associate them with and not their literal meaning. When we awaken, the left-hemisphere is back online, so the images in the dream become literal to us and do not make sense.

DREAMS REFLECT THE WAY WE THINK

Our dreams make use of schemas and scripts.[58] Schemas and scripts are a way of thinking about our world. We incorporate and process knowledge based on our experiences and preconceived ideas. These become our conceptual system.[59] For instance, we all have a schema for what a horse should look like. It should have a mane, hooves and a tail. When we see an animal that matches some of that criteria we compare it to our schema and decide if it is a horse also. Our dreams make use of our conceptual system of schemas and scripts by speaking in metaphors and figurative language.[60] The word metaphor means "transfer" in Greek.[61] A good example of the use of figurative language and metaphor is found in the Bible. Jesus often spoke in parables. He calls Christians "sheep" and himself a "shepherd." In this way, the abstract concept of his love is transferred to something we concretely understand. The idea is that metaphors transfer the meaning of abstract concepts like love and beauty into something we comprehend.

The right-side of the brain is in charge of providing metaphorical or symbolic thought for our dream content.[62] Figurative images relay an idea better than literal verbal expression. It is more impactful and memorable for me to tell you that "you are driving like a bat out of hell" than to say that "you are driving too fast." Our dreams make use of the same conceptual system of metaphors that gives us pictures of bats coming out of a fiery cave when we express disapproval of a spouse's careless driving. When people tell you that defining a dream symbol is highly personal, this is what they mean. Your metaphorical understanding of the images comes from your own unique way of thinking having been developed by your experiences. The fact that our dreams come from our memories and use figurative thinking developed by our experiences would suggest that they should be highly memorable, but counterintuitively they are not.

WHY DON'T I REMEMBER MY DREAMS?

Research has shown that we dream much more than we remember.[63] There are several reasons for this. It is thought that the mechanisms that control our working memory are not turned on when we sleep. We have no opportunity to consolidate our dreams. This means we do not transfer them from short-term to long-term storage.[64] Research also shows that the best predictor of whether or not a person remembers a dream is the attitude of that person towards dreams.[65] This means that people who think dreams mean something are the ones who remember them. Not all dreams are forgettable. In fact some of the most common dreams are the ones we remember in detail.

COMMON DREAMS

Although much of the content of our dreams is directly traceable to our memories, human beings have dreams that do not come from any known memory source. Dreams like flying, falling, being naked in public or having our teeth fall-out are common and found all around the world, but they obviously do not come from a memory.

Carl Jung tried to explain the fact that people have common dreams with his theory of the collective unconscious. It is now believed these dreams are part of a group of primary metaphors. Common dreams make use of our minds' ability to use figurative thinking.[66] We associate anxiety as teeth falling out. We associate fear as falling. We associate freedom or happiness with flying. We can understand this better by examining the system of non-verbal communication within facial expressions. There are facial expressions that can be understood no matter where you are. If you smile everyone associates that with happiness. If you furrow your eyebrows everyone associates that with anger. Crinkle your nose and that means disgust. Human beings make use of facial expressions to convey meaning without having to be taught. In the same way, our dreams make use of the metaphorical images of flying, falling and nakedness that we intuitively understand as fear, anxiety, happiness or embarrassment.

Although some of the most memorable dreams are common to humanity many of them cannot be attributed to our conceptual system. Their source seems to be external to the dreamer. Some dreams stay with us for a lifetime, others reflect a surreal quality about them. Nightmares and lucid dreams are two examples.

NIGHTMARES AND NIGHT-TERRORS

Nightmares are defined as a vivid dream containing overwhelming negative emotions wherein the participant is attempting to avoid some sort of threat.[67] It is estimated that nearly one half of adults have occasional nightmares and even more children.[68] Nightmares are different than night-terrors which occur during non-REM sleep and do not involve an accompanying dream, but a feeling of fear, anxiety or an evil presence.[69] In my experience, the general public does not differentiate between a nightmare and a night-terror; they lump the two together.

As a general rule, nightmares are traceable to real-life traumatic experiences and may closely simulate the actual event that caused them.[70] Because of this, some researchers argue that nightmares have to come from our declarative memories and not our implicit memory system.[71] If this is true, different types of dreams may retrieve their content from various places for reasons still unknown. Research has also shown that examining our nightmares is in fact less helpful to our psychological well-being then was previously thought.[72] Researchers found people to be better adjusted when they do not examine traumatic dreams for meaning or direction.[73] This finding was very controversial because many therapists teach traumatic dreams should be examined in order to garner emotional healing. They equate examining nightmares to looking at a picture that you find grotesque over and over.

Although some nightmares can be traced to our traumatic experiences, like a solider dreaming of war or a sexual assault victim dreaming of their attacker, much of our disturbing dreams do not have an obvious physical origin. For dreams like this it may be helpful to examine the controversial subject of lucid dreaming.

LUCID PHENOMENA

For centuries, lucid dreaming was mentioned in literature, but it wasn't until recently that science could prove its existence. As early as the eighth century A.D., Buddhist monks were taught to lucid dream in order to achieve enlightenment.[74] Achieving lucidity does not come naturally to most people. It has to be learned. Lucid experts teach how to induce this type of dream through various methods, including hypnotic and posthypnotic suggestion.[75] These methods are a way to prime your mind to keep certain areas active during dreaming that are normally turned off (executive control functions). This allows the dreamer to consciously create the content in the dream. Although lucid dreams share similarities with other types of dreams, there is some research that suggests it may be a higher level of consciousness.[76] What this means is that lucid dreams may be more similar to wakeful fantasizing than dreaming. Researchers who study lucid dreams classify biblical dreams as lucid because of the level of awareness, and goal-directed thought and behavior exhibited within them.[77] It may be that dreams from God activate executive control functions that normal dreams do not in order to engage the "ego" or "self" of the dreamer and transfer the dream to long-term memory.

My experience with people claiming to be lucid dreamers suggests their motives for wanting to control their dream environment comes from a desire to act out sexual fantasies. They report encountering dream entities that I would categorize as demonic spirits and they are conditioned to attempt to speak with them.[78] My advice is not to attempt to achieve lucidity because of its similarity to astral projection and spirit guided meditation.

CONCLUSION

If you wanted to know how the heart worked you would read an anatomy and physiology book. Trying to explain the inner workings of the body without it would be conjecture. The same is true for dreams. Our knowledge of the dreaming brain is superficial, but expanding exponentially. Because of this, it is wise not to be overly dogmatic, but we should embrace the best supported evidence. I do not want people to think I am ambivalent about my work defining dream symbols. These conclusions apply only to dreams that come from our mind. They do not reflect my opinion about dreams from God.

1. A basic knowledge of the physiological and cognitive processes of the mind is necessary for understanding dreams.

2. The majority of our dreams can be understood as a form of mind-wandering while asleep. This doesn't mean they are pointless. This only infers they are not as profound as once believed.

3. Because our dreams have continuity with our waking concerns many of them have a transparent meaning.

4. Examining every dream for meaning may not be fruitful or necessary.

3

FOUNDATIONS OF A
NEW FRAMEWORK

The current Christian literature is filled with books from powerful prophets who have done a magnificent job of covering what the Bible says about dreams. Authors like James Goll and John Paul Jackson. Because of this, I do not need to write comprehensively. My purpose for this chapter is to show the biblical foundations of the new framework including a critique of the position against a demonic source for our dreams. This is important because we are living in a time when God is calling out to people in dreams.

"It will come about after this that I will pour out My Spirit on all mankind; and your sons and daughters will prophesy, your old men will dream dreams, your young men will see visions." Joel 2:28

The devil knows God uses dreams to speak with people. This is why he has attempted to flood the marketplace with lies and confusing information. If you read secular dream books you will see the enemy trying to change the definitions of dream symbols in his favor. People are told that dragons are symbolic of good fortune and snakes speak of new beginnings.[1] The secular dream dictionaries directly contradict God's definitions of these things and the result is people are greatly misled. Many of the people who practice dream interpretation interpret solely as a means of turning people away from the truth.

> *"...Is there anything in the hearts of the prophets who prophesy falsehood, even these prophets of the deception of their own heart, who intend to make My people forget My name by their dreams which they relate to one another, just as their fathers forgot My name because of Baal? The prophet who has a dream may relate his dream, but let him who has My word speak My word in truth. What does straw have in common with grain?"* Jeremiah 23:26-28

The good news is that the Bible gives us objective criteria for establishing God's authorship of a dream. Although the purpose and function of dreams from our mind is debated, there is no debate about what a dream from God is designed to do. We are supposed to examine and act upon dreams from God. Dreams from God are prophetic. They are designed to give us insight, revelation and direction. Because of this they are easily distinguished from a dream from our mind. I call dreams from God "true dreams."

TRUE DREAMS

In Daniel 2:45 we see the prophet tell King Nebuchadnezzar that his dream was "true". Daniel does this as a way of differentiating it between other types of dreams. In Jeremiah 23:25-32 we see examples of dreams that were interpreted and given to people as if they had come from God. If we use the Bible to verify the source we can avoid assigning God's authorship to dreams that do not come from Him. Below I have delineated four qualities that distinguish a dream from God from another source.

1. They are memorable.

"Joseph remembered the dreams which he had about them..." Genesis 42:9

In the account of Joseph's dream in Genesis 37 we see that Joseph is seventeen when he has his dream. We later see in Genesis 41:46 that he is thirty when he enters the service of the king. This means that when Joseph recalls his dream, a minimum of thirteen years have passed and it could be as many as twenty. All dreams from God work this way. Seven years before I met my wife the Lord showed her to me in a dream. I remember it in detail to this day. If the dream is poorly remembered or vague it cannot have come from God. Unlike dreams from our mind they are transferred into long-term memory.

2. They are didactic.

"I will bless the Lord who has counseled me; indeed, my mind instructs me in the night." Psalm 16:7

"Then He opens the ears of men, and seals their in-struction," Job 33:16

Dreams from God must instruct us. They teach and edi-fy us. Many of the dreams in the Bible have a clear pur-pose. I call it a "can't miss the point" quality. Let me show you an example of not being able to miss the point of what God wants you to do.

"In Gibeon the Lord appeared to Solomon in a dream at night; and God said, "Ask what you wish Me to give you." 1 Kings 3:5

When people tell me they had an impactful dream. I tell them that is a good sign. I then ask if it gave them di-rection or an answer about something and it becomes ob-vious that the dream lacked a didactic quality. I see God speak to people openly in dreams just like the one in 1 Kings. In the dream I had in which God told me to create my website I was specifically asked about it. God does not always speak so plainly, but all of God's dreams have di-rection, instruction or revelation in them.

3. They are coherent.

"He had a dream, and behold, a ladder was set on the earth with its top reaching to heaven; and behold, the angels of God were ascending and descending on it. And behold, the Lord stood above it and said, "I am the Lord, the God of your father Abraham and the God of Isaac; the land on which you lie, I will give it to you and to your descendants." Genesis 28:12-13

Examine the dreams in the Bible. There is an organization to them that is readily distinguishable from dreams from our mind. God is a logical and intelligent being who is trying to communicate with people who are made in his image. Therefore, dreams from God must be coherent. This quality becomes apparent when dreams from God are contrasted to those that we know have come from our mind.

4. They are holy.

"You shall be holy, for I the Lord your God am holy."
Leviticus 19:2

People relate dreams to me that involve graphic descriptions of sex, violence and bodily functions, but these things violate God's holy character. The Bible contains many stories about prostitution and drunkenness, but they are not the same as some of the graphically disturbing dream images produced by the brain. God certainly does not try and shelter our eyes from the negative aspects of humanity, but the difference is in the amount of details we get. I recall a dream in which a woman said she was examining her own fecal matter. She wanted to know what it meant. I would hesitate to assign God's name to something like that. The dreams and visions depicted in the Bible do not contain feces, urine or pornographic images. If I were to tell you God has rabbit ears and rides a motorcycle you would ask me to show you scripture to support it. We should do the same when developing a theory of dreams.

I make a conscious effort to ensure my dreams do not violate these four objectively defined measures before I assign biblical meaning to them.

DREAMS FROM THE MIND

Most of the Bible deals with dreams from God. Because of this we do not have an abundance of scripture on the nature of dreams from the mind. However, there are verses that establish several key characteristics about them.

1. They are easily forgotten or recalled in fragments.

"He flies away like a dream, and they cannot find him; even like a vision of the night he is chased away." Job 20:8

This is the most distinctive quality of a dream from the mind. The verse in Job leads us to believe dreams are forgettable, but not all of them are, so which ones is he talking about? We have already seen that dreams from God are not forgotten. Chapter Two showed that most adults have between four to six dreams per night and forget 95-99 percent of them. Assume you are an average dreamer and have five dreams a night. If you remember one every morning and write it down you have an exceptionally high recall. One out of five would leave you remembering 20 percent of your dreams. This is far higher than average, but still means 80 percent of your dreams are forgotten.

Dreams from God are designed to be examined. Most of our dreams are forgotten. Therefore, the majority of our dreams do not come from God. They are produced by the mind and forgotten in the morning. This does not mean that dreams from God are rare or infrequent, quite the contrary. It simply means the only dreams we remember have the potential to be from God.

2. Continuity

"A hungry person dreams of eating but wakes up still hungry. A thirsty person dreams of drinking but is still faint from thirst when morning comes." Isaiah 29:8 NLT

The verse in Isaiah confirms the scientific finding that there is a transparent connection between dreams and a person's waking concerns. The man in Isaiah is hungry and thirsty. The time he spent thinking about his needs created anxiety which contributed to the creation of the dream. The continuity feature alone does not guarantee that a dream came from the mind. Dreams from God are frequently an answer to a person's concerns, but a transparent connection with our waking life is one of the key distinguishing features of dreams from the mind.

3. Bizarreness

"The heart is more deceitful than all else and is desperately sick; who can understand it?" Jeremiah 17:9

"...is there anything in the hearts of the prophets who prophesy falsehood, even these prophets of the deception of their own heart, who intend to make my people forget my name by their dreams..." Jeremiah 23:26-27

These verses speak of the deceitfulness of our flesh, its wants and desires. Dreams from our own fleshly desires do not follow the logical progression that a dream from God does. Because dreams from the mind are a mixture of the desires of our heart, thoughts and emotions, they can appear disorganized and incomprehensible. An example of the characteristic of bizarreness is a dream a girl related in which she and her friends walked around her hometown eating and talking while an enormous pair of blue jeans hovered in space above them. I recall another dream a young man had. In it he was eating breakfast at his kitchen table when a giant head of cabbage sat down next to him and the stick of butter on the table began speaking to him. These two dreams typify the quality of bizarreness and readily expose themselves as coming from the mind.

When examining your own dreams wait and see if the memory of the dream fades throughout the day. If you forget it by evening it may not have come from God. Ask yourself if the dream matches any of the things you did the previous day. Lastly, if the dream looks random and incomprehensible it is unlikely to be from God. The last source of our dreams is demonic spirits.

DEMONIC DREAMS

This is actually a controversial topic. I have spoken with Christians who vehemently deny demons can affect our dreams and they chastise me as naive for believing they can. Because of this I think it necessary to show the reasons I take this position.

I recognize this as an appeal to the people, but it is foolish to ignore the anecdotal accounts of those who say their nightmares are caused by demons. I have personally spoken to many of them. In Chapter One we showed that the ancients believed they were speaking with demons via dream incubation. This practice can still be found today, across many cultures[2]. You cannot go to Africa or India and tell the locals that wicked spirits cannot cause dreams.

You're credibility will be questioned.

The most common objection I hear to this position is there are no Bible verses supporting it. This is not true. To start, I would like to make a list of things commonly agreed upon that the Bible teaches us demons can do. This list is not exhaustive, but it can give us a proper perspective of the power that God's created intelligences possess.

1. Demons can cause sickness and disease, Luke 9:39.

2. Demons can possess people, Mark 5:9.

3. Demons can cause signs and wonders and make statues speak, Revelation 13:3, 13-15.

4. Demons can send negative thoughts into a person's mind, Ephesians 6:16.

5. Demons can pose as angels, 2 Corinthians 11:14.

If demons can do all of these things why is inducing a dream too difficult for them?

More biblical support can be found in Job. In Job 2:6 we are told that Satan is the culprit of Job's trouble including the death of his family and the loss of his property. In Job 7:14 he goes on to say he is suffering from terrifying dreams. Because God tells us in the beginning of the book that Satan is the cause of Job's problems, it is logical to conclude that Satan is also the cause of Job's nightmares. The dreams could not come from Job's own mind because in the same verse he says "you frighten me." If the dreams do not come from Job's own mind and Satan is not the cause, they would be the one thing in all Job's distress and misfortune God personally decided to inflict upon him. Why would God do this?

Another verse I want to examine is Jeremiah 27:9. There we see "dreamers" listed with false prophecy, fortune-telling and sorcery. The Bible teaches that fortune-telling, false prophecy and sorcery are activities caused by demons. Placing dreamers in the context of this list establishes them as being inspired by demons as well. Another way to look at this is by creating a hypothetical grocery list. Say your spouse asks you to go to the store and purchase items from the list below. You examine the list and notice an item you have not seen before called "kiwano."[3] Although you may not know what a kiwano is, you do know the rest of the items are fruit, making it a strong possibility that "kiwano" is one as well. The list in Jeremiah 27:9 acts the same way.

The wife's grocery list

Strawberries	False prophets
Oranges	Fortune-
Bananas	telling
Apples	Sorcery
Kiwano	Dreamers

Why are "dreamers" in a list of activities inspired by demons if it is not one also?

Another objection I hear is there are not enough verses to support taking a strong position that demons can be the cause of a dream. Do you know how many verses there are that directly state you should not murder? There are three, Exodus 20:13, Matthew 5:21 and Matthew 19:18. How many times does God need to say it?

To continue, I would like to examine what we know about the anatomy and physiology of the brain with regard to certain maladies. Chapter Two revealed the limbic system in the temporal lobe, and visual and auditory association cortices of the brain to be critical for dream formation. I would also like to introduce a familiar story from the Bible. In Mark 9:14-29 Jesus has come down from the Mount of Transfiguration. He encounters his disciples and heals a boy suffering from a "deaf and mute spirit." This spirit also causes the boy to have epileptic seizures. This story establishes that a demon caused deaf muteness and epilepsy in this boy. This begs the question: what does deaf muteness and epilepsy have in common with dreams? Deaf muteness affects the hearing and language centers of the brain in the temporal lobe.[4] Epilepsy affects this region and other forebrain areas involved with the formation of dream content.[5][6][7] The story in Mark proves demons manipulate and cause malfunction to regions of the brain vital to the formation of dream content. To accept the story in Mark and deny that demons can affect our dreams is like believing that a thief could break into your house and turn on your television but denying they had the intelligence to turn on the stove. If they can do one, they can do the other. The story in Mark supports this.

To sum up, we have scientific evidence revealing the areas in the brain associated with seizures and deaf muteness to be the same as those that affect our dreams. We have biblical evidence connecting a type of dreamer with a list of known demonically-inspired activities. Lastly, we have thousands of years of human experience and archeological evidence that confirms the widely held belief that demons can be the cause of a dream. The position that the Bible does not present scripture in support of demons being the cause of a dream is erroneous and maintaining that position contradicts both the Bible and the best scientific evidence.

Because we have biblical evidence supporting the position that demons can cause a dream, we can evaluate those qualities. Although I do not have a verbatim report on this type of dream, we can make inferences based on what the Bible tells us about the character of demons.

1. Intimidation

Demonic dreams use fear and terror to intimidate. Dreams from God can be fearful also, but not in the same way. In the account of Abraham's dream in Genesis 15 it says "terror" fell upon him. The difference between this and demonic terror is God was showing Abraham information about the oppression his descendants would incur and it scared him. Demonic dreams use terror to intimidate.

The enemy likes to use intimidation against God's people. The giant Goliath would taunt and intimidate Israel in order to demoralize them. When I began witnessing to people I had a dream that was designed to intimidate me so I would quit. In the dream I remember attempting to enter a dark room in an unknown building. When I entered the room blackness shrouded everything except for the feet of the people sitting there. When I started to talk to them about Christ a dark force tried to overwhelm me and push me out the door. When I awoke, I could tell the enemy wanted to shock me into believing he was too strong to be beaten. God had to strengthen and encourage me in His might so the seed of doubt would disappear and I could continue in the work of evangelism. Dreams with fear, terror and dark colors typify those of demonic origin.

2. Sexual perversion

"Yet in the same way these men, also by dreaming, defile the flesh, and reject authority, and revile angelic majesties." Jude 1:8

The verse in Jude is in context with the sexual practices of the people of Sodom and Gomorrah. Sexually perverse dreams are not the same as dreams with sexual content. It is not uncommon for people to dream of a tryst with an ex-lover. Those dreams come from the mind. The type of perversion associated with demonic dreams is that of bestiality or incest. I spoke with an adolescent male who confided he dreamt of having sex with a sheep. The young man was distraught because he had never been sexually active. I told him the dream was from a spirit of sexual perversion and if one of his older brothers was involved with pornography, it could have allowed it into the home. I also remember speaking with a group of men who told me they allowed a friend to stay with them while that friend was looking for a place to live. These men said the night their friend came to stay; everyone in the house had sexually perverse dreams. The friend admitted he struggled with a spirit of lust. They were able to pray for him and no one experienced troubling dreams afterwards.

3. They contradict God's word.

The verse in Jude also teaches us that demonic dreams reject authority. Any dream that contradicts God's word should be ignored. Demons lie to people in dreams. I remember the dream of a man who was told he was disqualified from participating in a prayer ministry at his church. He was approached in the dream by an unsavory character who showed him pictures of all the drugs and sexual misconduct he had participated in before becoming a Christian. The dream character told the man he was not holy enough to be involved with intercessory prayer. Because intercessory prayer does great damage to the enemy, this dream was an attempt to keep this man from participating in a powerfully disruptive ministry. This young man was able to submit the dream to other Christians who assured him that because the dream contradicted God's word it was not of the Holy Spirit.

If you see a dream that uses fear and terror to intimidate, contradicts the authority of God's word or has sexual perversion in it, do not assign God's authorship to the dream.

CONCLUSION

The evidence presented in this chapter clearly shows support for the three tenets of this framework. Most significantly, dreams originate from three different sources: The mind, God and demons. This chapter has also shown that dreams from our mind and dreams from God differ substantially in both objective and subjective criteria. Lastly, an examination of the quantitative differences between dreams from our mind and dreams from God establishes the fact that most dreams do not come from God. These findings must not be treated as trivial. They must be incorporated and acted on when examining dreams. In the next chapter we will couple these findings to objective principles in order to extract the meaning of dreams.

4

PRINCIPLES
OF
INTERPRETATION

This chapter incorporates principles gleaned from various disciplines to aid in an objective analysis of dreams. I believe dream interpretation is an art and a science as well as a gift. Ultimately, the best way to interpret dreams is to pray and rely on the Holy Spirit to guide your answers. After all:

> *"...Do not interpretations belong to God?"* Genesis 40:8

THE NEED FOR VALIDATION

The subject of dreams is surrounded by conjecture and religious mysticism. The devil likes it that way. Secular dream analysis is rooted in a combination of the beliefs of Sigmund Freud and Carl Jung.[1] Jung developed his beliefs by speaking with a demon in his dreams. Secular theories teach us to examine dreams from our mind for revelation, insight, and direction, but the Bible only endorses we listen to dreams from God. The inspiration of man provides little sustenance.

"What does straw have in common with grain?" Jeremiah 23:28

We need to be objective in our search for meaning because relating a dream is a subjective experience. Human beings make mistakes. People leave out important details. They may be embarrassed by something that happened in the dream. Many Christians do a fantastic job of carefully assigning meaning to their dreams, while others struggle to differentiate the ones they have. Alarmingly, I have encountered a number who think every dream they have is from God. This is not what is being taught, as this quote from James Goll states:

"It is not necessary always to spiritualize everything. Sometimes there is no spiritual content. Sometimes a dream is just a dream."[2]

Human beings look for reasons why we are right. We do not look for reasons why we are wrong. Researchers call this tendency a "confirmation bias."[3] One of the ways we can validate our dreams is by looking for reasons why we are wrong. If you want to avoid basing a life-changing decision on a dream from your mind, establish the source by using disconfirming evidence. This is the same method used by chess Grandmasters. They focus on where a move might be weak while novices look for reasons why a move is strong.[4] We can do the same.

LOOKING FOR BLACK SWANS

Prior to the discovery of Australia people in the Old World were convinced that all swans were white.[5] After all, they had seen millions of confirmatory sittings of white swans. Luckily for us, someone eventually found a single black swan. This lone observation invalidated the centuries old conventional wisdom that only white swans existed. In this way, we can see that not all pieces of information are equally important when looking for truth. We get closer to the truth with one piece of counter-factual evidence than with millions of instances of verification. In this case, not all swans are white. You can look for black swans while examining your dreams as well.

Look for disconfirming evidence by using the objective criteria presented in the last chapter about the nature of God-given dreams. See if the dream you are evaluating violates any of them. This will lead you to the true source.

1. God is holy.

Dreams with body fluids like pus, blood, feces and sexual content are well represented within the general population.[6] I recall a dream in which a girl confided she pulled tape worms out of her genitalia. Dreams like this represent the minds' way of mentally purging negative emotions, but they are not from God. I had a young woman tell me a dream which started with her in her local church, singing and dancing with other Christians. The dream progressed to religious dialogue between her and the other girls. I quickly started to think the dream had come from God. She then related that the end of the dream was a scene of her and her boyfriend engaging in a shockingly detailed, pornographic episode. The majority of the dream looked like a dream from God. It was memorable, it was logical, it had a religious theme, and until the end, it was Holy. Counter-factual evidence at the end disconfirmed God as the author. This dream was not a way for God to reveal this girl's sexual activity. If He wants to do that it will not look like an X-rated movie.

Because God is holy does not mean that all dreams with crass features come from our mind. I once dreamed that a friend and I were working at church shoveling sheep dung and some of it splattered on us. We were frustrated, but we could not get out of the work we were doing. Although a pile of sheep feces was in the dream, it was from God. He was telling us we would be doing hard, dirty jobs around the church, picking up after other Christians and there was no way out of it. Although there are some exceptions, the overall context of the dream must reflect God's holy character.

2. God does not contradict the Bible.

Dreams in which a person is told to commit ungodly actions eliminate the Holy Spirit as the source. This sounds easy, but the devil is subtle and our emotions can convince us that a dream came from God. An example of this is a dream in which a man was told to ask for supernatural help in taking revenge upon people who were harassing him at his job. The man had been praying about his work situation, but God says vengeance belongs to him and we are to forgive people who mistreat us. The advice he received in the dream led him to conclude that it was not from God. For this reason, test the spirits.

"Beloved, do not believe every spirit, but test the spirits to see whether they are from God..." 1 John 4:1

3. God is not violent or sadistic.

If you see a dream with rape or grotesque violence you can rule-out the Holy Spirit. Remember the three "S" rule. If a dream is sadistic, sinful, or abusively sexual, you can eliminate God as the source. Let me add the caveat that many end-of-the-world dreams are from God even though elements of violence are depicted. These dreams are terrifying to the dreamer, but you can identify them as coming from God because they are a depiction of what is written in the book of Revelation. In other words, they look similar to what God has already told us would happen. Applying these rules will quickly reveal the true source of a dream. Once you have confirmed the source you can interpret it.

WORKING WITH DREAMS

If the dream came from God you must use the Bible. Dreams from God are authored by the Holy Spirit. He gets to determine the meaning. If the dream came from the mind, it must be explained as a process of the mind. Dreams from the mind are a form of thinking while asleep. The dreamer is the author and applying biblical meaning to the images may actually mask the true meaning.

Have you ever used a Bible concordance? There are two definitions for most of the words in the Bible. One is in Greek and the other is in Hebrew. I have found myself attempting to understand the definition of a word only to realize I was trying to define an Old Testament Hebrew word while in the New Testament Greek section. Interpreting dreams is the same way. Applying a dream from your mind to a biblical definition is like defining a Hebrew word in Greek. It doesn't mean the same thing. Let me show you by interpreting some dreams with biblical symbolism then by explaining it as a dream from the mind.

"I had a dream that I was looking in the mirror, my lips were scabbed and my teeth were falling out. I just remember being stressed out."

The Bible is clear that teeth are symbolic of a person's words, Psalm. 57:4, Amos 4:6 and Psalm 3:7. This person also had diseased lips, which symbolize a person's speech, Isaiah 6:5. If the dream came from God, He is revealing something about their choice of words. Fortunately, the character of this person was not that of someone who gossiped or used profanity, and they admitted they had been stressed about a cold sore on their mouth. Because this girl is not a wicked person, it is likely the lips and teeth represent a cognitive metaphor for cold sores and stress. Applying biblical symbolism would have misled this person into thinking God was mad at her. Another example:

"I dreamt I went walking in my neighborhood and came upon a pond. I stopped and went fishing. Some of the fish where oddly colored and shaped."

The Bible says Jesus will make us "fishers of men" in Matthew 4:19. If this dream came from God, this man is going to be witnessing to the people around him. The reality is the man who had this dream admitted he was an avid fisherman and had been contemplating going to a lake the day before the dream. The dream lacked directions and dialogue and the man said it felt emotionally bland. These are good indicators that the dream came from his mind. With these examples, you can see how the source drastically changes the way we understand it. In order to avoid the pitfall of assigning biblical meaning to a dream from the mind, ask questions. One of the most common mistakes people make is not asking any questions or asking the wrong ones. Don't rush into an interpretation. I think this is foolish. Even though physicians are experts, they do not diagnose without talking to the patient first.

"He who gives an answer before he hears,
It is folly and shame to him." Proverbs 18:13

1. Focus on the dream holistically.

If you have ever been to an art gallery you know that the paintings are displayed to be viewed at certain distances. Dreams are the same way. If you see a single symbol you recognize, don't wrap a story around it. This is like sticking your nose on a painting. All you will see is one feature and your interpretation becomes myopic. Here's how it works.

"I had a dream where my friends and I were walking and talking with each other. In the dream my friends had red coats on, but mine was blue. We talked for some time then stopped and went in separate directions. I went to a lake shore nearby and looked out at the sunset. I sang and watched the birds and the fish. The whole dream was really peaceful."

Nose-on-painting interpretation:

"Blue means wisdom, so you are the only wise one in the group."

One of the differences between experts and novices is that experts quickly decipher between relevant and irrelevant information. Novices focus on isolated facts while experts try to understand problems holistically.[7] If you only recognize one feature of the dream, ask more questions before jumping to a conclusion about the meaning. People with little experience interpreting dreams can tell you that snakes are bad and the number seven stands for completion or perfection. Armed with the knowledge of a few dream symbols it becomes tempting to focus solely upon them while ignoring the rest of the dream. Focus on the dream as a whole and ask the right questions.

2. Ask the right questions.

Have you ever taken your car to a mechanic because it wouldn't start? When the tow-truck dropped it off how would you react if the mechanic started by trying to fix your paint job? Because he was focused on irrelevant information you might think he didn't know what he was doing. The best way to avoid getting focused on irrelevant information is not to assume every dream is spiritual in nature.

Most people come to me because they do not have a clue what their dream means. The first question I ask after listening to their dream is if it relates to anything in their life? As we saw in Chapters 2 and 3 the majority of our dreams come from our waking concerns and social interactions. If a person can match the content with something from their life the meaning becomes transparent. For example. I had a man relate a dream in which his brother became furious at him for looking through his possessions. The man confessed he had argued with his sibling while at a family function. By asking if the dream seemed similar to a lived experience the connection with the argument became apparent.

If you cannot determine what the dream means by listening to it, ask about the emotions. Remember, many people have a difficult time accurately relating a dream which may conceal the true meaning, but they will not forget the dominate emotions within it. Our emotionally charged memories and concerns are the ones we dream about. The emotions of stress, fear, sadness, pleasure and anxiety will frequently reveal more about the nature of a dream than the images. If the emotional content of a dream is negative I know to pray for joy and peace in that person's life even if the dialogue reveals very little.

Start off by asking the right questions. Don't assume every dream is spiritual. Resist the temptation to extract meaning from isolated facts and don't let minor details become the focus of your investigation.

3. Don't worry about details.

If you can understand the general meaning of a dream, give a minimalist answer. Sometimes an explanation of every detail distracts from the message. A good example:

> *"A vision appeared to Paul in the night: a man of Macedonia was standing and appealing to him, and saying, "Come over to Macedonia and help us." When he had seen the vision, immediately we sought to go into Macedonia, concluding that God had called us to preach the gospel to them."* Acts 16:9-10

Paul dispels with the details of interpreting this man's clothing, the way he was standing and how many straps were on his sandals, with the simple conclusion that God was telling them to go to Macedonia. I am not saying that detailed explanations of dreams are unnecessary (read the book of Daniel). What I advocate is not getting bogged-down. When I interpret the dreams of others I focus on the essentials. When you work with the dreams God has given you personally, it is fine to use a detailed system of analysis, but don't obsess over them for weeks.

4. Set time limits.

I speak with people who spend weeks or months praying about a dream to garner revelation. Remember, you are like Daniel. You are not like King Nebuchadnezzar who could not understand a God-given dream. The Spirit of the living God is in you. When God gives you a dream, He wants you to understand and act on it. Frequently, I see God give people the meaning of a dream the moment they wake up. I believe we should write down our dreams, pray about them, and wait for answers, but only for a set time. If the meaning of a dream does not come to you, ask someone else. If they do not understand it either, the silence of the Holy Spirit may be a tacit implication that the dream did not come from Him.

5. Ask for help.

"Let two or three prophets speak, and let the others pass judgment." 1 Corinthians 14:29

Dream interpretation for Christians is a way for the Holy Spirit to speak through you to edify someone else. Because of this I work with other Christians to avoid making mistakes. Although I write iconoclastically, I love, and support Christians who interpret differently than I do. When it comes to evangelism I like to think the color of the cat does not matter as long as it catches mice. I have friends who use Old Testament Law when evangelizing. I do not think this is best, but it is not worth arguing about. Dreams work the same way. There are many other authors and opinions on the subject. We think of dreams as a highly private matter, but whether you're witnessing or evaluating your own dreams it's wise to work in tandem. A humble and submissive spirit will keep you from making mistakes by deferring to others.

6. Read other authors.

I started interpreting dreams after I saw videos of John Paul Jackson. I then read what other authors had to say and incorporated those things into what I do. In this way, one person plants and another waters, and we are built-up in Christ. It is vitally important that we utilize the anointing of other Christians so the body is fully functional.

> "...God has allotted to each a measure of faith. For just as we have many members in one body and all the members do not have the same function, so we, who are many, are one body in Christ, and individually members one of another. Since we have gifts that differ according to the grace given to us, each of us is to exercise them accordingly..." Romans 12:3-6

Use these principles to guide your thinking when examining dreams. Eliminating mistakes increases your credibility. No one is perfect, but when you claim to speak prophetically and you make a mistake people do not let you forget it. It is my experience that people will let you pray for them if you interpret their dream correctly. Prayer finalizes the conversation allowing God to move in the life of the dreamer, but this also brings you into the realm of spiritual warfare.

THE MINISTRY OF INTERPRETATION

I have been fortunate to sit under the tutelage of many spiritual giants. The prophetess Cindy Jacobs of Generals International is a member of Trinity Church and speaks to us regularly. Trinity also teaches spiritual warfare classes under the expert guidance of another prophetess named Lisa Swayze. I have greatly benefited from both of these impactful ministries and the things I write about in this next section derive from those encounters.

Interpreting dreams is a powerfully impactful way to evangelize. The Holy Spirit speaking through you to another person is a form of prophecy. This ministry yields dramatic results. When you take your gifts into the marketplace of the world to witness be aware of several things. Most significantly:

1. You will be attacked.

Demons think people are their property. They act as though they are protecting a possession. This is understandable. If someone came into my house and attempted to steal from me I would fight. Here's an example:

> *"But if I cast out demons by the finger of God, then the kingdom of God has come upon you. When a strong man, fully armed, guards his own house, his possessions are undisturbed. But when someone stro-*

nger than he attacks him and overpowers him, he takes away from him all his armor on which he had relied and distributes his plunder." Luke 11:20-22

Jesus makes spiritual warfare analogous to breaking into someone's house and taking their valuables. I remember listening to a story from a powerful apostle about being physically choked by a demonic spirit the night he entered a particular region in an Asian country to pass out gospel tracts. He said power from heaven shot into his body to enable him to throw the spirit out of his tent. When you witness, you are attempting to take someone out of the direct control of the kingdom of darkness. Because of this your prayers have to be two-fold. You must pray that God's will be done in that person's life and you must practice binding and rebuking.

"I will give you the keys of the kingdom of heaven; and whatever you bind on earth shall have been bound in heaven, and whatever you loose on earth shall have been loosed in heaven." Matthew 16:19

You can pray and ask that God's will be done in a person's life, but if you want to drive the enemy out you must also bind and rebuke them. But in order to do this you need the help of other Christians.

2. Don't do it alone.

"Again I say to you, that if two of you agree on earth about anything that they may ask, it shall be done for them by My Father who is in heaven." Matthew 18:19

"Furthermore, if two lie down together they keep warm, but how can one be warm alone? And if one can overpower him who is alone, two can resist him.
A cord of three strands is not quickly torn apart."
Ecclesiastes 4:12

Information learned from failure is great non-charlatanic advice. It guarantees you know what will not work. I made the mistake of attempting to do everything by myself when I started evangelizing. I rebuked the enemy at every opportunity and prayed for many people on a daily basis. I learned that rebuking works, but demons are vindictive. Because of this, I suffered tremendous spiritual-warfare dreams every night for weeks. I would have dreams in which I was fighting multiple demons of different rank and size and I was getting overwhelmed. I was exhausted during the day because I lost sleep. The Holy Spirit had spoken to me clearly during this event and told me that although I had experienced warfare in the past it was not on this scale and I would not win. In my zeal I had bitten off more than I could chew.

I was taught not to quit a fight just because I was experiencing a little pain so I marched through the days and nights of wrestling. Although I was not fighting smartly, the Lord did not abandon me, but continued to give me revelation. The Lord showed me in a dream where the enemies in my area had called in specialists to deal with me. The wicked spirits in the dream were a type of special force that roamed around. Reluctantly, with the advice of some friends in the church I was able to retreat from the tactics of Rambo evangelism. Although I lost this battle, in the end the Lord showed me how it only takes a few Christians to produce powerful results.

"Then Jonathan said to the young man who was carrying his armor, "Come and let us cross over to the garrison of these uncircumcised; perhaps the Lord will work for us, for the Lord is not restrained to save by many or by few." 1 Samuel 14:6

It was also around this time that the Lord convinced me to start fasting more often.

3. Fasting and prayer.

Fasting and prayer are weapons of mass spiritual destruction.

"But this kind does not go out except by prayer and fasting." Matthew 17:21

"Is this not the fast which I choose, to loosen the bonds of wickedness, to undo the bands of the yoke, and to let the oppressed go free and break every yoke?" Isaiah 58:6

Many people do not like to fast, but the fact is some demons will not leave unless you fast and pray. Again, I learned this painfully. I like to worship Jesus and pray loudly. I ask for the salvation of every person in the city where I live. I have found that the devil does not like us asking Jesus to save people. My loud prayers get me into fights. On one occasion I felt strong opposition to my prayers for several days. The resistance continued even at night. I could not sleep without being constantly awakened by a demonic strongman. The Lord told me I was "in a war" and He allowed me to see the spirit. It appeared as a male figure about six feet tall, as bright as lightning. It had sharp iron fangs in its mouth, a serpent's tongue and it spoke with a gruff voice. Fortunately I was fasting at the time and the Lord led me to the book *Territorial Spirits* by apostle C. Peter Wagner. For those of you not familiar with the book, the title sums it up. Demons have territories they are tasked with controlling just like an army at war. The main job of demonic armies is to prevent Jesus from being glorified in their sector, which is why I was attacked. I was new to that town and this spirit was the welcoming committee. The entire event took about eight days of intermittent fasting and prayer, with the help of others, before God removed the strongman and spirits under him. The difference afterwards was a tangible quiet and blanket peace that can only be spiritually appraised. Through this experience I learned the enemy is terrified of God fighting on our behalf.

> *"Now the dread of the Lord was on all the kingdoms of the lands which were around Judah, so that they did not make war against Jehoshaphat."* 2 Chronicles 17:10

Since this time, I have great confidence that if you endure through the event, God will eventually defeat your enemies. If you want to minister to others by interpreting dreams be prepared to wrestle with the enemy.

4. God is looking for some wrestlers.

Several years ago Bill Johnson of Bethel church in Redding, California came to Trinity and spoke. During the message he talked about God looking for wrestlers. This call to arms was very encouraging. It resonated with me because of the work I was doing. I had begun to question if my militant attitude was sanctioned. After all, I was experiencing constant warfare. Bill's words confirmed to me that God wants Christians to engage the enemy. He's looking for opportunities to defeat the devil. You don't need to be a perfect Christian to be used. You simply need to be willing.

"For our struggle is not against flesh and blood, but against the rulers, against the powers, against the world forces of this darkness, against the spiritual forces of wickedness in the heavenly places." Ephesians 6:12

"Every place on which the sole of your foot treads, I have given it to you, just as I spoke to Moses." Joshua 1:3

When I am involved with a spiritual battle, the Holy Spirit will give me dreams revealing the names of demonic strongmen in the area. He will do this for you also in order to help you know what to pray. If you are not familiar with intercessory prayer, I recommend reading apostle Dutch Sheets' book *Intercessory Prayer*. It is where I learned the in-depth principles of prayer and the confidence to engage the enemy in that realm of ministry.

In Dutch's book, he shows us that the Hebrew and Greek words for "tread" have violent connotations. In Joshua 1:3 "tread" literally means "load your weapons."[8] God is telling us that wherever we are willing to take-up arms against the enemy, He is willing to fight for us. If God has given you the gift of interpreting dreams, He will also give you the victory when you step-out and wrestle with the enemy.

CONCLUSION

Interpreting dreams shouldn't become an exercise in pedantry, but we need to be more objective in our search for meaning. Dreams from the mind can look similar to dreams from God. The devil is also busy trying to manipulate people through the use of dreams. Examining our dreams is biblically sanctioned and encouraged, but acting on dreams from our mind is not. To avoid this, look for aspects of a dream that do not represent God's character. Compare and contrast the qualities that differentiate all three types of dreams and you will be able to correctly identify the source. Once you have identified the source of a dream, use the most appropriate system of interpretation to assign meaning to it. If the dream came from God, you must use the Bible. If the dream came from the mind, it can be understood as a cognitive process. If the dream came from a demonic source, use the principles of spiritual warfare to stop the enemy's plan. Ultimately, prayer allows God to assess your conclusions about the dreams you interpret.

5

INTERPRETING DREAMS

In this chapter I allow the reader to consider exemplars and use the theoretical knowledge from the previous chapters to interpret them. In order for true learning to take place, you must use what has been taught. Case studies close the gap between learning and doing. I have chosen these dreams specifically because they represent a prototype for every source of our dreams. There are many subcategories of dreams within each of these sources, but those are not covered in detail. The main focus is to allow you to correlate the concepts presented in this book with practical experimentation. I will begin this chapter by dividing the dreams by their source so the reader may become acclimated to seeing typical examples from each category. At the end, I allow the reader to sample dreams that have not been pre-categorized and interpret them without my modeling. Use the three steps of interpretation as you read and answer the questions in this chapter.

The three steps of dream interpretation

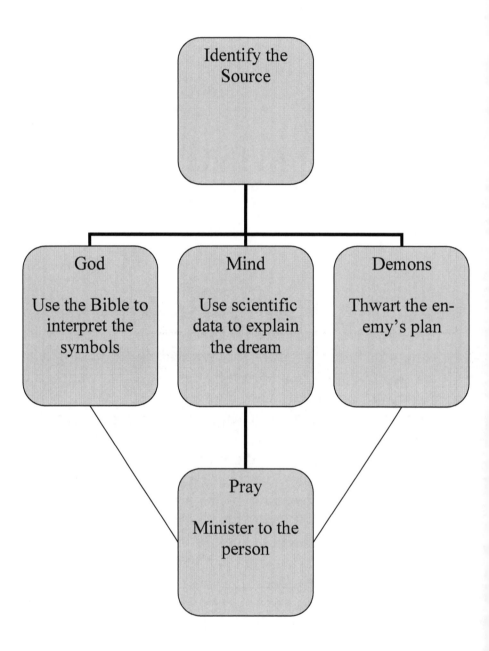

MIND

"I dreamt about a girl I work with that I really like. We were in my house sitting on the couch and she started kissing and touching me. It got really graphic and we ended up doing some weird sexual things that I would never do, but when I woke up I felt so in love with her that I think the dream meant something."

You can rule-out God as the source of this dream because of the graphic sexual content. When we dream our minds do not distinguish between real and imagined sex. This is why he awoke with strong feelings for his co-worker. The executive control centers of his brain are suppressed. The letting go of his self-control is why he acts-out sexual things he would not normally do. It is likely this dream is a result of a preoccupation with a girl he likes.

"I had a dream where an apple and a bird were sitting together reading a book at the library. They started to argue and the bird picked up the apple and threw it into the mouth of the librarian. She ate it, said it tasted great then spit the seeds into the ground. Then she buried them with a hoe and danced on top of it."

This dream is bizarre, but it does not contain anything unholy. Also, I do not see a logical or clear purpose to the dream. For these reasons, it is unlikely to be from God.

"I dreamt I was at the North Pole with my family. While we were sitting around a fireplace a polar bear came to the window and started talking. I asked my brother if there were any other animals around, he showed me a penguin and a fish."

The person dreamt of this during the Christmas holiday season. Because the dream does not contain the didactic qualities of a dream from God it is reasonable to say the dream came as a result of this person thinking about their holiday experience.

"I had a dream there was something nasty like cauliflower growing out of my hair. In the dream I decided to cut it out using a kitchen knife. All I remember is that I felt stressed out and uncomfortable at the whole thing. Then I woke up."

This dream is bizarre, but it is not incoherent. The emotion is the important clue to why this girl had the dream. She is experiencing a stressful time in her life. Remember, the emotional centers of the brain are highly active and may play a large role in what we dream about.

"I dreamt I was throwing red balls in the air. I threw bright red balls up in the air and then caught them. As I was doing this I saw someone next to me holding blue and green balls, but they never said anything."

I would like to point out the brevity of the dream and its lack of an obvious teaching principle. If you use the Bible to interpret this dream it becomes incoherent. For example, blue means wisdom, green means life and red can mean anger or perhaps the blood of Christ? Interpreting the colors does not give clarity to the dream. The person next to her does not give us any details either. It is unlikely this dream came from God.

"I keep dreaming of my young son speaking to my husband and I while we are playing with him on the living room flo-

or. I hear my son speak in plain English. It seems so clear, but I cannot remember what he is saying specifically."

If the woman from this dream could remember something specific her infant son said, it could be important. Because she cannot, the dream is likely from her mind.

"I am really suspicious of my husband having an affair because I keep dreaming of him cheating on me. In my dreams I keep seeing him with other women. I wake up mad and angry at him. I don't recognize the woman in the dreams, but I feel like they work with him."

This dream is common when there is a compulsive preoccupation concerning the fidelity of a spouse. If a man or woman has experience infidelity this type of dream will recur.

"I had a dream all my teeth kept falling out of my mouth and were horribly cracked when I looked in the mirror. I was so full of anxiety; I just kept staring in the mirror. I couldn't do anything about it."

If the dream was from God the teeth are symbolic of the dreamer's words. The dreamer is not the kind of person that spouts acerbic or vicious things; her mind is making use of metaphorical images to express her anxiety.

"I had a dream about the number 364. I thought God was telling me to play the lottery or something. I also dreamt that the number 19 was on my wall so I went to the book of Revelation and read the nineteenth chapter. What does this mean?"

When the dream comes from God the meaning of the number is without question. The most common mistake when seeing numbers in a dream is associating them with a random book or chapter in the Bible upon awakening. If God wants you to look up a verse He will not just give you the number 19. He will give you chapter and verse as well.

"I dreamt I was talking to my friends in a house and then it switched to me driving a car with my family. My mom was driving really fast and I was yelling at her to slow down. We ended up at the mall and I saw a guy I like. He was with a girl from school I hate and it made me jealous. I started fighting with this girl in front of some friends and no one helped me. I sat down and started crying asking God for help."

Although the end of the dream is a religious scene the rest is a reflection of her daily life, social concerns and family dynamics. Because of this it is unlikely God gave her the dream. This girl is a Christian and frequently attends church. Because of this, elements of her spiritual life will be expressed in dreams from her mind.

"I dreamt I could see the moon and night sky in vivid detail. I have never seen them so clearly, they were so beautiful. I just stared at them. I was stunned by the details I could see in the moon, then all of a sudden a shooting star came across the sky."

When we dream, the mind utilizes complex imagination capabilities. It is able to do this without distractions because external sensory input is turned off. This is why dream images appear with telescopic clarity. This should not be seen as profound.

GOD

"I was in a boat rowing really hard by myself and these black flying things were pushing one side of the boat. It felt like I was going to flip into the water and drown. They were also trying to steer me towards a dark place on the water and I was getting tired. I started to pray, pleading for Jesus to help me and when I was about to capsize, bright lights appeared out of nowhere, chased away the black flying things, picked up the boat and took me to some calm water."

The boat and the struggle in the water represent this man's difficultly in trying to live a Christian life. The black flying things are demonic. The bright lights lifting him to safety is the divine intervention initiated by his prayer. They are angels. The dream was given to him so that he could pray and God would help him garner peace in his life, which is symbolic of the calm water. The dream was remembered by this person years afterwards and contains directions for his life in-line with the character of God. For these reasons it is safe to act upon the dream.

"Years ago I was given a gospel tract by a group of Christians. I read it and did not think much about it until later that night when I had a dream. I was really old and eagerly waiting, looking in the sky for something. Just then I saw a bright light flashing across the sky and started to scream and yell 'he's coming back, he's finally coming back.' I woke-up screaming the same thing and could not calm myself down for the entire day."

This dream was remembered twenty years afterwards. It is obvious this man has a call to accept Christ. Because the dream matches what we know about the second coming of Christ we can conclude this dream came from God.

"I had a dream where my sister and I were brought to some otherworldly place where we saw God. God looked at us and told us that we needed to go back to earth and try to bring as many people to Him as we could. My sister and I flew to earth in a ball of fire and landed near our friends and family. We tell them that we saw God. I kept begging them to come with me because the world was about to end, but they would not listen. My sister and I start to walk around and tell people to come to heaven with us, but everyone says they don't believe us. They say they want to stay where they are. I woke up feeling sad."

Only the Holy Spirit would tell someone that they needed to lead people to Christ before the end-of-the-world. This dream was remembered by this person in detail years after the fact and contains a clear purpose and direction. Because of this it is safe to make a decision based on this dream.

"I had a dream I was in my grandparent's house. I looked out the back sliding glass doors to the open road and saw five tornadoes coming at the house. I panicked because they were destroying everything. I immediately heard the voice of God come out of the sky and tell me to walk outside and command the tornadoes away from the house in the name of Jesus. I did and they fizzled into nothing."

Tornado dreams can mean two different things. Tornadoes can either be the signature of the presence of God or trouble brewing in someone's life. The context of the dream makes it clear these tornadoes are trouble. The end result was that this person felt led to pray for his family when he awoke.

"I was standing by a road looking in the distance when I saw a huge storm coming. It looked like a tornado. I waited and when it arrived I knew God was in the back of it. I woke up and the Holy Spirit impressed upon me that God was going to make an appearance in my life that would bring the change I had been waiting for."

Here we see another tornado dream, but this time the context makes it clear that it is symbolic of the presence of God.

"I had a dream where I died and went to heaven. When I got there I saw a giant golden city. People were carrying baskets full of fruit and food and coming in and out of the gates. I looked and saw Jesus waving at me inviting me into the city."

The girl who had this dream was an adolescent and had not accepted Christ into her life. I told her the dream was an invitation to accept Christ as her savior. It is noteworthy that the dream contained no dialogue, but communicates clearly. In this case, interpreting the symbols of the golden city, fruit and food is not needed to extract the meaning.

"I had a dream there was a huge black snake with a dark blue cross on its head under the seats of our church. I was the only one who seemed to notice the snake. It would try to change color and hide every time I pointed at it. In the dream I would try to tell people about it and warn them not to sit near it, but they ignored me."

This dream dictates this woman can see spiritual trouble within her church and no one is listening to her. God gave her the dream so she could pray and expose these problems. The dark blue cross is symbolic of a spirit of anti-Christ or false religion.

"I had a dream where my sister and I were climbing a very large mountain with a dark sky as the backdrop. The mountain had steps leading all the way to the top with scriptures on them. We were very tired, but we kept going. Every time we stepped on a stone the scripture would illuminate the path ahead."

The siblings are being shown how to navigate life. The climb is symbolic of moving progressively forward. The scripture is symbolic of God's word leading them and giving them light for every step. The darkened sky gives the sense that life is not easy right now; they may be emotionally upset about their current situation. The dream is very obviously from God. His signature is on every aspect of the dream giving it a "can't miss the point" quality.

DEMONS

"For most of my life I have had recurring dreams of being chased by a hooded figure. In my dreams I'm walking around looking at dead people. Then a dark hooded figure comes out of nowhere, grabs me, starts choking me and tells me 'God can't help you.' I always wake up in a panic."

The statement at the end indicates the hooded figure is a demon. The recurring nature of the dream is not unusual in that familiar spirits will continue to seek out individuals over the course of their life unless they are forced to leave them alone permanently. In this case, you would bind and rebuke the enemy, commanding it to leave in the name of Jesus. If this person does not change their lifestyle the spirit will return.

"I dreamt that my little brother and I were in our room and this big black snake with a red marking on its back is attacking us. My brother tries to fight, but he keeps getting bitten over and over. I try and help him, but we can't beat the snake, it keeps coming back."

The dream is a representation of a spiritual battle taking place in this boy's life. The snake is a demon. The red marking on its back identifies what kind of spirit it is. It is a spirit of anger. Variants of this kind of battle in the home are common. You will see a familiar spirit take the form of a lizard or a spider in many dreams.

"I had a dream last night that I have not had in many years, but it was definitely familiar. In my dream this evil spirit keeps pulling me towards a direction that I don't want to go. I scream in my mind, but nothing comes out of my mouth. In the dream I can't get away and I can't speak. I try and pray to God and eventually I wake up terrified. It seems so real."

This dream is a night-terror it is not the same as a nightmare which does not have to be demonic in origin. Night-terrors occur on the threshold of sleep and wakefulness. The signature of a night-terror is the inability to speak or scream and a feeling that some entity is near you. This dream was most certainly caused by a demonic force.

"I have a recurring dream where I am in water. It can be the ocean, a pool or a lake, but the same shark is eating people. This shark is relentless, it doesn't eat me, but I see it coming after my family members. I feel terrified in the dream because the shark jumps and eats my family even when they get on a boat or dry land."

The shark is destroying this person's family, but not him. The fact that his family is attacked while on dry ground indicates they feel they are in a safe place, but in reality they are not. The recurring nature of the dream indicates this is a continual attack of the devil on this family.

"I dreamt that I was lying in bed and out of the corner of my eye I see this black figure with horns and red eyes. It jumps on me and forces me to have sex with it. I try to fight, but I can't move or scream. I feel violated."

Sex with animals, family members or mystical figures identifies a spirit of sexual perversion to be the cause of a dream. A rape by a devilish figure is more common with women, but I have encountered men who sheepishly admit to being forced to copulate with a demon in a dream.

"My husband and I recently found out that I am expecting a child. I had this weird dream where we are walking around a dark castle and this witch with blackish blue eyes approaches us and begins to tell me things about the future. I don't remember everything she said, but she wanted to help us make decisions about our child. I agree and she starts touching me inappropriately and speaking in some weird language I can't understand then it ends."

The dream is an attempt to influence the direction of this couple's life. It is not uncommon to have a demon approach someone in a dream and give them ungodly advice. Ostensibly benevolent spirits that speak to people in their dreams are referred to as "spirit guides" by the general public. The woman who had this dream admitted she was involved with New Age practices. This would explain the dream.

"I am currently living with my aunt and uncle. My cousin is about to come and stay with us while he is out of school. I had a dream I was walking around their house. I walk into the room where my cousin is going to live and in the corner I see a golden spirit sitting with its eyes closed like it is meditating. My cousin has some weird religious beliefs and the spirit looked like a Hindu god."

The golden spirit is a spirit of false religion. The dream is showing the young man that his cousin's religious beliefs have allowed this spirit to take up residence in the house.

"When I was eight or nine my parents moved to a new house. The first night I dreamt the door to my room started to glow and then slammed open. A dark green mist crept up the stairs into my room then a womanly figure floated up the stairs. She had a greenish hue and shimmering silver dress. She stopped and looked at me. I was scared to death. Her form was beautiful, but she looked evil like she was dead. She pointed at me and snarled that I had "awakened her" and then slowly sank back down the stairs. I will never forget this dream."

Demonic dreams can be memorable. This dream was caused by a familiar spirit that resided in the house. In my experience demonic spirits are territorial. They will attempt to intimidate people or scare them out of an area like a dog protecting its territory. I have heard stories about spirits that growl. People understand growling. It means "I'll bite if you don't leave." This dream was an attempt to intimidate this boy into living with fear.

MISCELLANEOUS

"I had a dream last night that my mother and I robbed an outlet mall near our house. My mom had a gun and hijacked a city bus after we robbed the mall to take us home. She told the driver to drive to our house. When the driver took off I looked out the back window and we were being chased by thousands of dogs. Then the dream ended."

What's the Source?

Interpret the Dream.

"I had this dream that starts with my wife and I walking the streets of our city. We look towards the sky and see thunder and lightning forming in the clouds above. Rain starts to pour and a huge wave as tall as a building crashes on top of us. We find ourselves underwater, but I'm surprised that we can breathe. I feel like we are dead and tell my wife to come to the surface. When we come to the top of the water the scene switches to us on a cruise ship. She and I walk around the ship where everything is peaceful and calm, but I can't escape the feeling that we are dead."

What's the Source?

Interpret the Dream.

"I had this amazing dream where I met a guy I've never seen before and we fell in love. The strange thing was my really annoying friend introduced us. They were dating, but he left her and followed me to my room. We sat on my bed and started making out. I could feel every kiss. It was great. I think this guy is the one for me, but I've never met him in real life."

What's the Source?

Interpret the Dream.

"This dream scared me to death. I was in a desert, surrounded by dead bodies. The sky was red and all the trees looked like they had been burnt. I looked and saw a mushroom cloud in the sky behind me, but I did not hear any noise. I saw that I was covered in blood. I turned around and saw that my family was dead. I had killed them by choking them. I felt anguish. I somehow knew the end-of-the-world was happening and I couldn't escape it."

What's the Source?

Interpret the Dream.

"I had this dream that my teeth were being worked on by a dentist. He made them look perfect. In real life my teeth are uneven, but I'm alright with that. In the dream the dentist stopped before he was finished. I left and went to a party with jacked-up teeth, but I wasn't embarrassed."

What's the Source?

Interpret the Dream.

"I had a dream last night that I was with a group of several hundred soldiers being marched into an old gothic church. We go inside and a gunfight breaks out with some bad guys. I hit the floor and roll under a pew. When the bullets stop flying I look up and see an old priest opening a giant book with stained glass depictions of the end of the world on the front of it. There was more to this dream, but that is all I remember."

What's the Source?

Interpret the Dream.

"About fifteen years ago I had a dream where I was driving around my town. I stopped in the parking lot of a church. In a tree next to one of the parking spots was a dove that kept beckoning me to follow it into the church. In my dream I somehow knew that the dove wasn't really a bird it was like a spirit. When I got inside the church the dove landed on a book and then disappeared. I walked over to the book and picked it up. The whole church lit up with music and lights. It was the most peaceful song I had ever heard. I remember the words from the song were 'he cares, he cares, he really cares for us'. I am not religious, but I felt very spiritual in the dream."

What's the Source?

Interpret the Dream.

"I had a really strange dream last night. I was swimming in my pool and I look above my house and see a Buddhist monk. He is sitting cross-legged floating in the air. He opens his eyes, smiles at me and floats high into the sky with these huge dragon wings and then disappears. When I look back towards my house I see that he has left an egg with a serpent inside it on my roof."

What's the Source?

Interpret the Dream.

"I have a recurring dream. It has happened three times that I can remember. In my dream there is a really big house. When I go inside I sit down and see all of my dead relatives. My mother, my aunt, my grandfather, they are in the living room talking to each other, but they ignore me like they did in real life. I am so angry at them for ignoring me in the dream that I storm out of the room slamming the door to the house behind me."

What's the Source?

Interpret the Dream.

"I had a great dream last night where my friends and I were at a Justin Bieber concert. He pointed to me and called me on stage with him. He took me backstage and we held hands while we walked to his car. I am a really big Justin Bieber fan and I have always wanted to meet him. Does this mean I am going to meet him in real life?"

What's the Source?

Interpret the Dream.

"In my dream vampires were killing everyone in my town. If you got bitten you would turn into a vampire with color- less eyes and no emotions. My girlfriend and I were trying to stay together as we avoided vampires. We hitchhiked down a dusty road and one of my friends pulls up in a truck. We get in and drive away, but a vampire fly's through the back window, grabs my girlfriend and takes off with her. I felt helpless and guilty. I didn't tell my friend to turn around and try and get her."

What's the Source?

Interpret the Dream.

"I had a dream where I went to a psychic reading with some voodoo looking old lady. She described some people to me that I do not get along with in real life. I started to get nervous in the dream. She went to her shelf, mixed two things together, sprinkled them on me and said an incanta- tion. She then told me to drink some potion. I felt better af- ter I drank it, but I felt intent about getting revenge on the two people she had described. In the dream I blamed them for my anxiety. I paid the lady some money that looked like gem stones, then the dream ended."

What's the Source?

Interpret the Dream.

"My mother, brother and Jesus were in a dream I had last night. We were at Six Flags theme park on a roller coaster and I was watching my mother and brother from the ground. I turned to one of the people in costume that take pictures with you, he took his rabbit head off and it was Jesus. He gave me a cookie and walked away."

What's the Source?

Interpret the Dream.

"I am going on a family vacation soon and last night I dreamt that my family and I got on a plane heading to some island that was supposed to be the greatest place. We boarded the plane and it took off fine, but when we flew through the clouds it started to shake. We looked in the cockpit and could see the pilots drinking beer. The plane started to fall apart and then it crashed. I think this is a warning or something?"

What's the Source?

Interpret the Dream.

"I have had really bad luck lately. I lost my job, my boy-friend dumped me and I am always depressed. Well, the other night I dreamt that I was driving my car down a pitch-black road really fast. I could feel myself being thrown around the car when I went around corners. I tried to push the brake pedal, but I had no brakes. I nearly crashed into a house. In my dream I looked on the hood and some black, ghostly thing was steering my car. I felt in the dream that it was the reason my brakes did not work. I kept screaming at it, but it just laughed at me. At the end of the dream I heard a voice in my head ask me if I believed Jesus could help and I screamed "YES" at the top of my lungs and then I woke up. I am not a religious person but I know this dream means something."

What's the Source?

Interpret the Dream.

"About a week ago my cousin Lilly had a dream where she and I were walking together with our families. She said that we started to skip and run, then we grabbed each other's hand and flew up in the air for a few seconds. We came back down to the ground and my mother said, 'Why don't you really try next time?' Lilly said we started running and flew as high as the clouds. She said she could feel the wind in her face and see the sun."

What's the Source?

Interpret the Dream.

"*I got into an argument with one of my co-workers the other day. Later that night I had a dream where he and I were shooting at each other with machine guns. Every time I shot him he would get smaller and smaller until he became a child. In the dream I kept shooting at him and when I woke-up I felt really awful about it.*"

What's the Source?

Interpret the Dream.

"*I have never had a dream where an animal spoke to me, but last night I dreamt that a black wolf followed me home from school and talked to me all the way. It told me that he would always be with me and I could ask him anything. In the dream I was asking him all kinds of questions and he could answer all of them. He was really smart.*"

What's the Source?

Interpret the Dream.

"I had a dream early this morning that I was watching a woman swimming down a river when she was attacked by a crocodile. The dream started over from the beginning, but the only thing that was different was that she was attacked by a lion. The dream repeated itself again and I became the woman in the dream. I was trying to swim away from the lion and just as it was about to bite me I woke up."

What's the Source?

Interpret the Dream.

"Last night I had a dream where I was sitting watching television and looked down at my legs and saw a giant sore on my knee. I looked closer at it and inside I could see pus and hair matted together. I felt disgusted but I cannot fathom what this dream means."

What's the Source?

Interpret the Dream.

"I had a dream where I saw my deceased husband stand-ing in front of me. He looked sad and started to cry. He was very sick when he died. My husband past away years ago, but I know the dream meant something because I was upset when I woke up."

What's the Source?

Interpret the Dream.

Notes

1. THE SCIENCE OF SLEEP

[1] *Why Do We Sleep Anyway?* (2013, 11 6). Retrieved from healthysleep.med.harvard.edu: http://healthysleep.med.harvard.edu/healthy/matters/benefits-of-sleep/why-do-we-sleep

[2] Fults, E. (2013, 11 13). *Inside Life Science: How Our Bodies Keep Time*. Retrieved from livescience.com : http://www.livescience.com/13123-circadian-rhythms-obesity-diabetes-nih.html

[3] Ibid

[4] *Sleep Research.* (2013, 11 13). Retrieved from The American Technion Society (ATS): http://www.ats.org/site/PageServer?pagename=about_sleep research

[5] Ibid

[6] Ibid

[7] *How long can humans stay awake?* (2013, 11 13). Retrieved from scientificamerican.com: http://www.scientificamerican.com/article.cfm?id=how-long-can-humans-stay

[8] Ibid

[9] (2013, 10 25). Retrieved from PsychCentral: http://psychcentral.com/lib/stages-of-sleep/0002073

[10] Ibid

[11] Ibid

[12] (2013, 10 24). Retrieved from University of Maryland Medical Center : http://umm.edu/programs/sleep/patients/normal-sleep

[13] Ibid

[14] Solms, M. (1997). *The Neuropsychology of Dreams: A Clinico-Anatomical Study.* Lawrence Erlbaum.

[15] Obringer, L. A. (2013, 11 6). *how dreams work* . Retrieved from how stuff works : http://science.howstuffworks.com/life/inside-the-mind/human-brain/dream3.htm

[16] Van De Castle, R. L. (1994). *Our Dreaming Mind.* New York: Ballantine . Pp. 228-287

[17] Schneider, A., & Domhoff, G. W. (2013, 11 12). *frequently asked questions.* Retrieved from dreamresearch.net: http://www2.ucsc.edu/dreams/FAQ/index.html

[18] Domhoff, G. W. (2002). *The Scientific Study of Dreams Neural Networks Cognitive Development and Content Analysis.* Washington: APA Press. p. 4

[19] Ibid, p. 4

[20] Ibid, p. 20

[21] Ibid, p. 22

[22] Ibid, p. 22

[23] Ibid, p. 22

[24] Van De Castle, R. L. (1994). *Our Dreaming Mind.* New York: Ballantine . Pp. 229-230

[25] Ibid, Pp. 241-287

[26] Ibid, Pp. 291-310

[27] Ibid, p. 285

[28] Ibid, Pp. 296-310

[29] Ibid, Pp. 296-310

[30] Ibid, Pp. 296-310

[31] (2013, 10 24). Retrieved from A BRIEF HISTORY OF SLEEP RESEARCH: http://www.stanford.edu/~dement/history.html

[32] Ibid

[33] Ibid

[34] Ibid

[35] Hobson, J. Allan, M.D. McCarley, Robert. W. M.D. . (1977). The Brain as a Dream State Generator: An Activation-Synthesis Hypothesis of the Dream Process. *The American Journal of Psychiatry* , Vol 134:1335-1348.

[36] Nielsen, T. (2013, 11 14). *Dream incubation: ancient techniques of dream influence*. Retrieved from dreamscience.ca : http://www.dreamscience.ca/en/documents/New%20conte nt/incubation/Incubation%20overview%20for%20website%2 0updated.pdf

[37] Ibid

[38] Ibid

[39] Ibid

[40] Domhoff, G. W. (2002). *The Scientific Study of Dreams Neural Networks Cognitive Development and Content Analysis*. Washington: APA Press. Pp. 135-136

[41] Van De Castle, R. L. (1994). *Our Dreaming Mind*. New York: Ballantine . p. 109

[42] Ibid, p. 128

[43] Domhoff, G. W. (2002). *The Scientific Study of Dreams Neural Networks Cognitive Development and Content Analysis*. Washington: APA Press. p. 135

[44] Ibid, p. 136

[45] Van De Castle, R. L. (1994). *Our Dreaming Mind*. New York: Ballantine . p. 109

[46] Ibid, p. 117

[47] Domhoff, G. W. (2002). *The Scientific Study of Dreams Neural Networks Cognitive Development and Content Analysis*. Washington: APA Press. p. 142

[48] Van De Castle, R. L. (1994). *Our Dreaming Mind*. New York: Ballantine . p. 165

[49] Ibid, p. 250

[50] Ibid, Pp. 140-143

[51] Ibid, Pp. 145-146

[52] Ibid, Pp.146-147

[53] Ibid, Pp. 146-147

[54] Ibid, Pp. 146-147

[55] Domhoff, G. W. (2002). *The Scientific Study of Dreams Neural Networks Cognitive Development and Content Analysis*. Washington: APA Press. p. 143

[56] Van De Castle, R. L. (1994). *Our Dreaming Mind*. New York: Ballantine . Pp. 160-161

[57] Ibid, p. 147

[58]Domhoff, G. W. (2002). *The Scientific Study of Dreams Neural Networks Cognitive Development and Content Analysis.* Washington: APA Press. p. 144

[59] Van De Castle, R. L. (1994). *Our Dreaming Mind.* New York: Ballantine . Pp. 156-157

2. A CONTEMPORARY VIEW OF DREAMS

[1] Allen R. Braun*, Thomas J. Balkin, Nancy J. Wesensten, Fuad Gwadry, Richard E. Carson, Mary Varga, Paul Baldwin, Gregory Belenky, Peter Herscovitch. (1998). Dissociated Pattern of Activity in Visual Cortices and Their Projections During Human Rapid Eye Movement Sleep. *Science* , Vol. 279 no. 5347 Pp. 91-95 .

[2] Franklin, Michael S., Zyphur, Michael J. (2005). The Role of Dreams in the Evolution of the Human Mind. *Evolutionary Psychology*, 3: 59-78 .

[3] (2013, 10 29). Retrieved from pbs.org: http://www.pbs.org/wgbh/nova/body/stickgold-dreams.html

[4] Cherry, K. (2014, 2 6). *Catharsis* . Retrieved from About.com Psychology : http://psychology.about.com/od/cindex/g/catharsis.htm

[5] (2013, 10 28). Retrieved from dreamscience.org: http://dreamscience.org/idx_science_of_dreaming_section-1.htm#1.1_Do_We_All_Dream

[6] William Oates Covington, J. (2014, 7 1). *Allan Hobson's AIM Model for Consciousness*. Retrieved from willcov.com: http://willcov.com/bio-consciousness/front/Hobsons%20AIM%20Model.htm

[7] Domhoff, G. W. (2002). *The Scientific Study of Dreams Neural Networks Cognitive Development and Content Analysis.* Washington: APA Press. Pp. 146-156

[8] Ibid, p. 151

[9] Ibid, p. 3

[10] Ibid, p. 169

[11] Ibid, p. 16

[12] (2013, 10 25). Retrieved from University of Toronto Media Room: http://media.utoronto.ca/media-releases/health-medicine/study-identifies-how-muscles-are-paralyzed-during-sleep/

[13] (2013, 10 26). Retrieved from About.com: http://psychology.about.com/od/nindex/g/neurotransmitter.htm

[14] (2013, 10 26). Retrieved from Sciencedaily : http://www.sciencedaily.com/articles/n/neuron.htm

[15] Jian-Sheng Lin, Olga A. Sergeeva and Helmut L. Haas. (2014, 7 23). *Histamine H3 Receptors and Sleep-Wake Regulation.* Retrieved from The Journal of Pharmacology and Experimental Therapeutics : http://jpet.aspetjournals.org/content/336/1/17.full

[16] Siegel, J. (2013, 10 27). Retrieved from The University of Iowa Department of Psychology : http://www2.psychology.uiowa.edu/Faculty/blumberg/Course_Docs/Seminar.2008/Readings/Siegel.REMSleep.pdf

[17] Ibid

[18] Domhoff, G. W. (2002). *The Scientific Study of Dreams Neural Networks Cognitive Development and Content Analysis.* Washington: APA Press. P. 3

[19] Kieran C. R. Fox, Savannah Nijeboer, Elizaveta Solomonova, G. William Domhoff and Kalina Christoff. (2014, 1 20). *Dreaming as mind wandering: evidence from functional neuroimaging and first-person content reports.* Retrieved from Frontiers in Human Neuroscience : http://www.frontiersin.org/Journal/10.3389/fnhum.2013.00412/full#h6

[20] Ibid

[21] Ibid

[22] Bloom, P. (2010). *How Pleasure Works: The New Science of Why We Like What we Like .* New York : W.W. Norton & Company, Inc., p. 156

[23] Ibid, Pp. 170-171

[24] Kieran C. R. Fox, Savannah Nijeboer, Elizaveta Solomonova, G. William Domhoff and Kalina Christoff. (2014, 1 20). *Dreaming as mind wandering: evidence from functional neuroimaging and first-person content reports.* Retrieved from Frontiers in Human Neuroscience : http://www.frontiersin.org/Journal/10.3389/fnhum.2013.00 412/full#h6

[25] Domhoff, G. W. (2011). The neural substrate for dreaming: Is it a subsystem of the default network? *Consciousness and Cognition*, 20, 1163-1174.

[26] Sousa, D. D. (2013, 11 13). *6 Major Parts of the Brain and How they Work.* Retrieved from How the Brain Learns: The Blog: http://howthebrainlearns.wordpress.com/2011/11/28/6-major-parts-of-the-brain-and-how-they-work/

[27] Mastin, L. (2013, 11 4). Retrieved from howsleepworks.com: http://www.howsleepworks.com/dreams_function.html

[28] Robert Hoss, M. (2013, 11 13). *Section 3 - The Neurology of Dreaming.* Retrieved from dreamscience.org : http://dreamscience.org/idx_science_of_dreaming_section-3.htm

[29] (2013, 10 29). Retrieved from Neuroscience online : http://neuroscience.uth.tmc.edu/s4/chapter06.html

[30] Ellenbogen, Jeffrey M, Payne, Jessica D and Stickgold, Robert. (2006). The role of sleep in declarative memory consolidation:. *Current Opinion in Neurobiology 2006, 16:716–722*, 16:716-722.

31 Leutwyler, K. (2014, 1 24). *Tetris Dreams*. Retrieved from Scientific American : http://www.scientificamerican.com/article/tetris-dreams/

32 Ibid

33 Nielsen, Tore A., Philippe Stenstrom. (2005). What are the memory sources of dreaming? *Nature, 437*, 1286

34 Leutwyler, K. (2014, 1 24). *Tetris Dreams*. Retrieved from Scientific American : http://www.scientificamerican.com/article/tetris-dreams/

35 Ibid

36 Nordqvist, C. (2014, 1 24). *What Is Amnesia? What Causes Amnesia?* Retrieved from MNT : http://www.medicalnewstoday.com/articles/9673.php

37 Leutwyler, K. (2014, 1 24). *Tetris Dreams*. Retrieved from Scientific American : http://www.scientificamerican.com/article/tetris-dreams/

38 Ibid

39 Domhoff, G. W. (2002). *The Scientific Study of Dreams Neural Networks Cognitive Development and Content Analysis.* Washington: APA Press. p. 144

40 Van De Castle, R. L. (1994). *Our Dreaming Mind.* New York: Ballantine . p. 260

41 (2013, 10 29). Retrieved from pbs.org: http://www.pbs.org/wgbh/nova/body/stickgold-dreams.html

[42] Ibid

[43] Domhoff, G. W. (2005). The content of dreams: Methodologic and theoretical implications. In T. R. In M. H. Kryger, *Principles and Practies of Sleep Medicine 4th Ed.* (Pp. 522-534). Philadelphia: W. B. Saunders.

[44] Domhoff, G. W. (2002). *The Scientific Study of Dreams Neural Networks Cognitive Development and Content Analysis.* Washington: APA Press. p. 69

[45] Hartmann, E. (1998). *Dreams And Nightmares: The Origin And Meaning of Dreams* . Cambridge : Perseus . Pp. 61-76

[46] *Dreams: Expert Q&A.* (2013, 11 14). Retrieved from pbs.org: http://www.pbs.org/wgbh/nova/body/stickgold-dreams.html

[47] Domhoff, G. W. (2002). *The Scientific Study of Dreams Neural Networks Cognitive Development and Content Analysis.* Washington: APA Press. p. 21

[48] Van De Castle, R. L. (1994). *Our Dreaming Mind.* New York: Ballantine . Pp. 253-255

[49] Wren, K. (2014, 2 10). *How the Brain Turns Reality into Dreams* . Retrieved from nbcnews.com: http://www.nbcnews.com/id/3077505/ns/technology_and_science-science/t/how-brain-turns-reality-dreams/#.UvkA8vldUdU

[50] Ibid

[51] Ibid

52 Hartmann, E. (1998). *Dreams And Nightmares: The Origin And Meaning of Dreams* . Cambridge : Perseus . xi

53 Robert Hoss, M. (2013, 12 11). *Section 3 -The Neurology of Dreaming*. Retrieved from dreamscience.org: http://dreamscience.org/idx_science_of_dreaming_section-3.htm#3.1__The_Dreaming_Brain

54 Van De Castle, R. L. (1994). *Our Dreaming Mind.* New York: Ballantine . p. 271

55 Ibid, p. 271

56 Robert Hoss, M. (2013, 10 29). *Frequently Asked Questions about Dreams*. Retrieved from dreamscience.org: http://dreamscience.org/idx_faq.htm

57 Robert Hoss, M. (2013, 12 11). *Section 3 -The Neurology of Dreaming*. Retrieved from dreamscience.org: http://dreamscience.org/idx_science_of_dreaming_section-3.htm#3.1__The_Dreaming_Brain

58 Domhoff, G. W. (2002). *The Scientific Study of Dreams Neural Networks Cognitive Development and Content Analysis.* Washington: APA Press. p. 29

59 Cherry, K. (2014, 1 20). *What Is a Schema?* Retrieved from about.com: http://psychology.about.com/od/sindex/g/def_schema.htm

60 Domhoff, G. W. (2002). *The Scientific Study of Dreams Neural Networks Cognitive Development and Content Analysis.* Washington: APA Press. p. 35

[61] Baker, S. (1973). *The Practical Stylist.* New York : Thomas Y. Crowell Company. P 83

[62] Robert Hoss, M. (2013, 12 11). *Section 3 -The Neurology of Dreaming.* Retrieved from dreamscience.org: http://dreamscience.org/idx_science_of_dreaming_section-3.htm#3.1__The_Dreaming_Brain

[63] Van De Castle, R. L. (1994). *Our Dreaming Mind.* New York: Ballantine . Pp. 228-229

[64] Robert Hoss, M. (2013, 11 18). *Section 1 - Sleep and Dreaming.* Retrieved from dreamscience.org: http://dreamscience.org/idx_science_of_dreaming_section-1.htm#1.5_Dream_Recall_

[65] Ibid

[66] Domhoff, G. W. (2002). *The Scientific Study of Dreams Neural Networks Cognitive Development and Content Analysis.* Washington: APA Press. p. 32

[67] Deirdre Barrett, Patrick McNamara. (2012). *Encyclopeda of Sleep and Dreams: the evolution, function, nature, and mysteries of slumber.* Santa Barbara: ABC-CLIO. Pp. 463-464

[68] LaBerge, S. & Rheingold, H. (1990). *Exploring the world of lucid dreaming.* New York: Ballantine Books. p. 137

[69] Deirdre Barrett, Patrick McNamara. (2012). *Encyclopeda of Sleep and Dreams: the evolution, function, nature, and mysteries of slumber.* Santa Barbara: ABC-CLIO. Pp. 463-464

[70] Nielsen, Tore A., Philippe Stenstrom. (2005). What are the memory sources of dreaming? *Nature, 437,* 1286

[71] Ibid

[72] *Sleep Research.* (2013, 12 17). Retrieved from The American Technion Society (ATS): http://www.ats.org/site/PageServer?pagename=about_sleep research

[73] Ibid

[74] Van De Castle, R. L. (1994). Our Dreaming Mind. New York: Ballantine . P 441

[75] LaBerge, S. & Rheingold, H. (1990). *Exploring the world of lucid dreaming.* New York: Ballantine Books. Pp. 2-3

[76] Lucid dreaming: a state of consciousness with features of both waking and non-lucid dreaming. (2009). *Sleep* , 9:1191-200.

[77] Van De Castle, R. L. (1994). Our Dreaming Mind. New York: Ballantine . Pp. 440-441

[78] LaBerge, S. & Rheingold, H. (1990). *Exploring the world of lucid dreaming.* New York: Ballantine Books. p. 147

3. FOUNDATIONS OF A NEW FRAMEWORK

[1] *dream dictionary* . (2014, 2 7). Retrieved from Dreammoods.com : http://www.dreammoods.com/

2 Van De Castle, R. L. (1994). Our Dreaming Mind. New York: Ballantine . Pp. 45-69

3 Kiwano is an exotic fruit from Africa

4 (2013, 10 30). Retrieved from The Brain: understanding neurobiology through addiction : http://science.education.nih.gov/supplements/nih2/addicti on/activities/lesson1_brainparts.htm#

5 (2013, 10 31). Retrieved from mayoclinic.com: http://www.mayoclinic.com/health/temporal-lobe-seizure/DS00266

6 (2013, 10 19). Retrieved from epilepsyfoundation.org: http://www.epilepsyfoundation.org/aboutepilepsy/seizures /

7 Domhoff, G. W. (2002). *The Scientific Study of Dreams Neural Networks Cognitive Development and Content Analysis.* Washington: APA Press. Pp. 3-4

4. PRINCIPLES OF INTERPRETATION

1 Domhoff, G. W. (2002). *The Scientific Study of Dreams Neural Networks Cognitive Development and Content Analysis.* Washington: APA Press. Pp. 134-135

2 Goll, J. (2006). *Dream language the prophetic power of dreams, revelations, and the spirit of wisdom* . Shippensburg: Destiny Image Publishers Inc. p. 122

[3] *Confirmation bias.* (2014, 1 23). Retrieved from http://www.princeton.edu/~achaney/tmve/wiki100k/docs/Confirmation_bias.html

[4] Ibid, p. 59

[5] Nassim, T. (2007). *The Black Swan: the impact of the highly improbable* . New York : Random House. xvii

[6] *dream bank* . (2014, 2 10). Retrieved from dreammoods.com: http://www.dreammoods.com/dreambank/

[7] Herr, N. P. (2014, 1 21). *2 How Experts Differ from Novices.* Retrieved from The Sourcebook for Teaching Science: http://www.csun.edu/science/ref/reasoning/how-students-learn/2.html

[8] Sheets, D. (1996). *Intercessory Prayer: How God Can Use Your Prayers to Move Heaven and Earth* . Ventura : Regal books . p. 73

Made in the USA
Columbia, SC
28 February 2019